W9-CFC-507

In My Heart I
Carry a Star

IN MY HEART I CARRY A STAR

CARRY A STAR

STORIES *for* ADVENT

DEREK MAUL

UPPER
ROOM BOOKS®
NASHVILLE

IN MY HEART I CARRY A STAR: Stories for Advent
Copyright © 2008 by Derek Maul
All rights reserved.

No part of this book may be reproduced in any manner whatsoever without written permission of the publisher except in brief quotations embodied in critical articles or reviews. For information, address Upper Room Books®, 1908 Grand Avenue, Nashville, TN 37212.

The Upper Room® Web site: www.upperroom.org

UPPER ROOM®, UPPER ROOM BOOKS®, and design logos are trademarks owned by The Upper Room®, Nashville, Tennessee. All rights reserved.

Unless otherwise noted, scripture quotations are from the New Revised Standard Version Bible, copyright 1989 Division of Christian Education of the National Council of the Churches of Christ in the United States of America. Used by permission. All rights reserved.

Scripture quotations noted NIV are from the HOLY BIBLE, NEW INTERNATIONAL VERSION®. Copyright © 1973, 1978, 1984 by International Bible Society. Used by permission of Zondervan Publishing House. All rights reserved.

At the time of publication all Web sites referenced in this book were valid. However, due to the fluid nature of the Internet, some addresses may have changed or the content may no longer be relevant.

Cover design: Bruce DeRoos / Left Coast Design
Cover image: © age fotostock
Interior design, implementation: Nancy Terzian / buckinghorsedesign.com
First printing: 2008

LIBRARY OF CONGRESS CATALOGING-IN-PUBLICATION DATA
Maul, Derek, 1956–
In my heart I carry a star : stories for Advent / Derek Maul.
    p. cm.
ISBN 978-0-8358-9966-6
1. Advent—Prayers and devotions. I. Title.
BV40.M39 2008
242'.332—dc22   2008015797

Printed in the United States of America

To Grace, David, Bob, Nelle, Fred, Connie, Arthur, and Lily . . .
all those whose clear witness has paved the way for me to know the
truth, and the grace, and the fullness, and the joy.

CONTENTS

ACKNOWLEDGMENTS

I can't talk about this new project without saying a huge thank-you to my wife, Rebekah, who encouraged me to follow my heart when it was time to say good-bye to classroom teaching. "Everything is possible for him who believes," Jesus pointed out (Mark 9:23, NIV). Rebekah has always believed well, and her belief is contagious.

At Upper Room Books my editor, Robin Pippin, has been an enthusiastic "yay" from the beginning; project manager Jeannie Crawford-Lee is a breath of fresh air; Jill Ridenour and Jeanette Pinkston exude confidence. Janice Neely, Karen Duncan, Rita Collett, Terrie Livaudais, Mary Lou Redding, and Anne Trudel have remained encouraging and true. Thanks to all of you for your dedicated work.

Literally hundreds of friends, readers, and encouragers consistently lend prayers and support that lift up everything that I do. I'll mention a representative few: Andrew, Naomi, Craig, Geoff, Gary (times two), Gerard, Peggie, Andy, Jerry, Darrell, the Davids, Tim, Kelly, Joyce, the Henrys, all the POGS, Wayne. . . . And, hey, if you're anywhere in the orbit of First Presbyterian Church in Brandon, Florida—members and friends alike—then take a bow: you nourish the spiritual life that enables me to say anything at all.

A Word to the Reader

This book is designed to serve as a kind of devotional almanac, a traveling companion for our Advent journey: a guide not only for Jesus-followers but also for those looking in from the periphery of belief. The following pages—more than just a collection of stories that help us understand the meaning of Christmas—ultimately turn out to be a personal statement of faith.

You'll find my family—Rebekah, Andrew, Naomi, and eventually her husband, Craig—splashed all over these pages. I can't help myself; I love them so much and they teach me every day. Then, and for the same reasons, you'll also discover my extended church family as well as a lot of my friends, and even the assorted collection of pets that have shared our home.

The people I care about and whose stories infuse my journey refuse to fit into any snug or easy-to-define category. They love God, and they try to follow Jesus; but other than that, they're pretty much all over the map.

- They are cutting-edge; they are traditional; they are divorced; they are emergent; they are single; they are married; they are confused; and they are widowed.
- They are committed, faithful, floundering, and hopeful.
- They are baby boomers; they are young; they are middle-aged; and they are elderly.
- They are liberal; they are moderate; they are conservative; and—more often than you'd think—they are at a loss to make up their minds.
- The people who inspire me are generous; they are forgiving; they are gracious; and they are deeply faithful too.

- They are of every color and every race; they are of every slice of humanity in between.
- They are confident in their faith, and they are searching for truth.
- They are unpredictably and often perplexingly assorted.
- They are, in fact, just like the all-encompassing, welcoming, hard-to-stereotype, and remarkably patient love of Jesus—a love that always and continually draws us all into the heartbeat of God.

I believe that you will recognize in these pages the Savior who unites us all, the Christ who desires to bless creation with an Advent journey overflowing with expectation and life and hope and love.

I want this expectant Jesus to challenge us too.

This is my prayer: that—in the midst of all the wonder, and the bustle, and the peace, and the constant performance art that is December—the Jesus who makes my life necessarily uncomfortable at times will work God's inexorable way out of the margins and into the heart of Christmas Present, for each one of us, with increasing grace and with everlasting peace.

> From his fullness we have all received, grace upon grace. The law indeed was given through Moses; grace and truth came through Jesus Christ.
> —John 1:16-17

—Derek Maul

FINDING MY TRUE CHRISTMAS SELF

Clap your hands, all you peoples;
shout to God with loud songs of joy.
    For the LORD, the Most High, is awesome,
    a great king over all the earth.

                                   —Psalm 47:1-2

Ready or not, we're coming up on another December; probably my favorite month in the year. Traditionally, I've had a hard time reconciling the way we do Christmas with my commitment to simply follow Jesus, but recently I've discovered increasing spiritual meaning in celebration. "But when the fullness of time had come, God sent his Son . . . so that we might receive adoption as children" (Gal. 4:4-5). What could be more exciting than that?

PUTTING ON THE SPARKLE

As of last year our house is dressed up in this whole new array of Christmas lights. Our kids can hardly believe how daringly festive we're getting. I remember when we used to wait until a week before Christmas Day to decorate anything. We'd throw one set of lights on a large houseplant, pull down our small box of decorations, and hang a wreath on the door.

"We're all about the spirit of Christmas," we told our deprived offspring, "but we don't have to do all that showy bling to make it work."

We certainly weren't Scrooges—no matter what our children may have been telling their friends. My wife, Rebekah, and I wanted to make sure our household latched onto the authentic seasonal message. We didn't want to be so distracted by glitz that the sparkle was all we could see. And that's just on the inside. Then there's the whole slippery slope of exterior lighting. How much is too much? Do we live in a neighborhood or on Disney Main Street? Where does it all end?

Every time the kids asked why our house looked so dull, we would roll out the following litany:

"Christmas doesn't have to be gaudy."

"Lights are too expensive."

"Roofs are dangerous."

"We don't want to short out the whole neighborhood like the people next door."

"We don't have to be just like everyone else."

"We have a lovely wreath for the front door."

It's not like we were against decorating, and over the years we gradually added carefully conceived ornamental elements. But our approach had always been low-key. I've never been anywhere near comfortable with "over-the-top." I'm a subdued, easygoing, low-budget kind of a guy. As actress Susan Sarandon said in the movie *The Banger Sisters*, looking self-critically in the mirror, "Everything that I own is beige."

BLITZKRIEG

Then, one year, the lid came off. Looking back, I can still relive the shock of arriving home from work early one December day to find my wife perched on the roof of our house. Her van was crammed with festive surplus; icicle lighting cascades hung from the gutters; extension cords ran every which way; the roof of our house looked like the main runway at Tampa International Airport. She must have put up five thousand lights, and she was just getting started.

I eased my way up the ladder and peered over the gutter. "What happened to, 'They're too expensive—it's too much trouble—we don't want to short out the neighborhood—it's dangerous—we have a lovely wreath on the front door?'" I asked cautiously.

"They're pretty," she said, as if that alone could justify anything. "Besides, I've always liked lights on the house." And that was that.

It was as if the dam had broken. The interior came next. Before I knew it there were two Christmas trees and an illuminated back porch.

Now the large tree in the family room holds the traditional ornaments we have accumulated over the years. The tree in the living room features just about every variety of angel ever imagined. Crystal teardrops refract the light.

I'm not sure, but last year by the middle of December I think pretty much the entire heavenly host had gathered to watch over the Nativity below.

The house is a riot of seasonal splendor and Christmas light. Candles, greenery, festive bows, garlands, wreaths, doorknob hangings; you name it. Seasonal tableware in the dining room; Christmas coffee mugs on the countertop; lightbulbs placed carefully under each specimen in Rebekah's glass-insulator collection.

We're big book people, and we display illustrated volumes—everything from O. Henry's *The Gift of the Magi* and Oscar Wilde's *The Selfish Giant*, to Rebekah's old family-favorite rendition of Luke's narrative, and a well-worn *The Night Before Christmas*.

Twelve large, elaborately costumed international Santa Claus figures sit on bookshelves and other places. Then there's the garrison of nutcrackers. Who knew there could be so many variations on one concept?

The air is thick with Christmas at our house. Incredibly, Rebekah always manages to pull it all together with impeccable good taste, balanced and livable; kind of a festive feng shui.

Our children, now young adults, can't understand what happened. "Why didn't we have all this stuff back when we were little? Have you completely lost your marbles?" I think they believe we had been sandbagging them all those years.

Personally, I wouldn't have it any other way. I've been liberated, as it were. Last year I was even seen wearing a silver bell and a loud sweater to a Christmas party. I have found my true Christmas self. Fact is, the coming weeks are a celebration worth going over the top.

Think about it. Consider what was at stake when God entered this dangerous world as a helpless infant. Reflect on the nature of the gift. Make a little more noise about it. Celebrate. I know I will.

A City Built on a Hill

Fact is we dearly love our festive Florida home. It's relaxed, it's welcoming, it's user friendly, and it puts people at ease. In short, it makes a perfect Christmas house.

But like most families, we lead busy, bustling lives, so the key word when we do make it home is *relaxed*. Sometimes it's just one of us plus the animals; sometimes it's the whole tribe; and sometimes our children bring home spares. Downtime is precious, so we have learned to come to terms with unfinished laundry, dust bunnies, piles of items that really should be put away, and the occasional sink full of breakfast dishes . . . or was it last night's dinner?

Consequently, it turns out to be a good thing we entertain as often as we do. There's nothing like the welcome promise of imminent guests to provoke a quick and efficient shakedown. "I don't know how you do it," people tend to gush as we try to look for all the world as if we're used to seeing the house decked out, shipshape, and shiny. "Your home always looks so beautiful."

Such was the situation one recent Saturday in late January. The blitz was on, and one of us caught sight of a rogue leftover Christmas decoration. It was a small angel, hanging gracefully from the dining room chandelier. The erstwhile ornament had avoided a series of roundups, but this time he was caught out in the open. I quickly scooped up the heavenly being and dumped him unceremoniously into a cardboard box marked "Christmas: Miscellaneous."

Hastily I placed the box in the garage and immediately experienced a distinct stab of guilt. I felt like the postholiday goon squad, fanatically dedicated to eradicating any remaining evidence of seasonal goodwill. I thought about how easily we pack away everything associated with December's grace and mystery, then park it all securely in some dark, forgotten place until next year.

December thoughtfulness doesn't nearly cover the tremendous sin of our ongoing indifference, and often we let the light burn down too easily. It takes more than a casual Advent observance to write the gospel of love on our hearts with any durability. What we need is an Advent journey that leads to both the manger and the Cross.

I couldn't help but remember two separate news briefs I had caught on the same day, just a few weeks after Christmas: "Good news for retail," the TV anchor cheerily reported, "personal spending has risen sharply in the fourth quarter." Then: "In the wake of several natural disasters," a voice on the car radio told me later that afternoon, "charitable contributions have been drying up due to nationwide 'compassion fatigue.'" The incongruity struck me hard, and I wondered whether Christmas makes any difference at all, or is just another party favor designed to be tossed aside on the way home, destined to dissolve in the first good January rain?

Theology while cleaning was giving me a headache, so I turned my attention to the task of vacuuming, cleaning kitchen countertops, and washing windows. Eventually the house sparkled with welcome for our guests. It always does.

When we had finished preparing for company, I made a pot of hot tea. Rebekah and I looked around. We realized how extraordinarily blessed we are, how amazingly rich. Rich in things, yes, but rich in family too. And we are rich in friends, rich in love, rich in faith, rich in devotion.

Yes, our children can be challenging, and our relationship is constantly—and sometimes reluctantly—a work in progress. But the affection, the peace, the love, and the generosity that reside in our home overwhelm me at times. Joy too; real, substantial, and laced with abiding hope right there in the middle of the January doldrums. I'm thankful for everything, so grateful to God, and thrilled with the promise that Christmas really can spill over into our new year.

I made my way back into the garage, rummaged around, and rescued our adventurous angel. I put him back on the chandelier. After all, he'd already held out for so long. More significantly, our "holdout seraph" is a cogent reminder of the holiday spirit, the spirit of Christ that should never be packed away, taped up, and stored in a dark place.

What did Jesus say about our reaction to his coming? How did Christ characterize the kind of life change God anticipates in response to the Advent of Hope, Peace, Love, and Joy?

"You are the light of the world." He was talking about me.

"A city built on a hill cannot be hid." He was talking about each one of us.

No one after lighting a lamp puts it under the bushel basket, but on the lampstand, and it gives light to all in the house. In the same way, let your light shine before others, so that they may see your good works and give glory to your Father in heaven.—Matthew 5:14-16

Week 1

HOPE

Prelude to Hope

Learning How to Follow a Star

In the time of King Herod, after Jesus was born in Bethlehem of Judea, wise men from the East came to Jerusalem, asking, "Where is the child who has been born king of the Jews? For we observed his star at its rising, and have come to pay him homage."

—Matthew 2:1-2

Most of us have great stories stored up in our experience. The narrative of our lives helps to define us and, if we look carefully enough, common themes emerge that say a lot about our identity and what makes us tick. Some of the stories are treasure stored safely in our hearts; some we pass on to our children; some are too embarrassing to ever let out of the safe, and others touch us so deeply that we want to share them with the world.

The following is one such tale that has become legend in our family. I have retold it many times, and it has been passed on by others. What took place in our house that Christmas placed Advent squarely in the realm of the interactive, exactly where the celebration belongs. The season of preparation is much more than a distant chronicle from ancient history; the truth of the story should engage our entire household, every day, if we are to latch on to the deeper meaning of Christ's coming, brand new and alive, every time December rolls around.

SERENDIPITY

I can't remember a Christmas when Rebekah and I failed to learn something profound about faith from our children. It happens without fail. But seldom has the lesson been any clearer than the memorable December our olive-wood Nativity display made the leap from tableau to live theater. Both Andrew and Naomi were in preschool—ages four and a half and two years, four months; they were the wise.

Family tradition, only a few years in the making, dictated placement of our rough-hewn manger scene close to the floor. We wanted the Christmas story present and accessible, so we placed the Nativity scene under our tree. Carefully positioned stars and angels hovered overhead on the lower branches.

That year—pretty much just as soon as we'd set out the whole Nativity—a terrible disaster befell the tranquil scene. Every last wise man vanished into thin air, along with their camels. Even the baby Jesus ended up missing.

Later we found the wise men, all together in a group at the far end of the house. Jesus was still unaccounted for, but we hoped he'd show up before long; we rescued the characters and put them back where we believed they belonged.

They disappeared again—same thing; then again—ditto; and once more the next day. I was getting irritated with the children and threatened to glue the Magi to their camels or tie them to the tree.

About the fifth night, just as I was about to read the riot act to our son, Rebekah pointed out the interesting fact that the little group of kidnapped figurines was actually making progress. If we were smart we'd leave well enough alone and see what happened.

I've got to admit that "leaving well enough alone" has never been a natural reflex for me. As a father, and as a husband, I've been too guilty far too often of stirring when I should have just let things take their course. I always tend to believe I can fix things, set things straight; you know— "I'm the dad! Just watch me sort it all out."

But this was one of those times I actually took a cue, and so I bowed to my wife's deeper spiritual intuition. Consequently we were treated to the most amazing stunt ever pulled by two children with a collective age of less than seven!

JOURNEY TO BETHLEHEM

Every day we woke up to find Melchior, Gaspar, and their friend Balthazar just a few feet closer to their destination. Sometimes the camels lagged behind but they'd quickly catch up. By the third week of Advent they'd all made it to the dining room, traveling with caution, close to the table legs or under a chair.

Sometimes it's best to experience Christmas without overanalyzing, but how I wish I would have thought to document the progress on film. Instead I found myself wrapped up in the unique journey—always west, it turned out—and both Rebekah and I were drawn inexorably closer to the Savior ourselves.

The day before the night before Christmas, our wandering tribe of stargazing scholars camped out in the open, and then they dashed past the patio doors as fast as they could before spending two whole days gazing earnestly at the growing pile of brightly colored gifts just to the east of the tree.

When we left for church on Christmas Eve, the group was still staring at the presents. They had ground to make up, and I wondered how the final act would play out. I wanted to hide somewhere and watch, so I planned to do just that before they went to sleep. But—miraculously— by the time we returned from church the entire tableau was somehow complete. And, Lord knows how the children pulled it off, Jesus himself was finally back in the manger.

WONDER

How a four-year-old could have stashed such a treasure so carefully and for so long I still can't say. How did he keep his secret, and how did he manage to get his sister to cooperate? It remains a mystery to this day.

But this I do know: my children's pantomimed expedition to Bethlehem created an awareness of my own journey that has never left me. When I am wise, I remember that no Christmas scene should ever resemble a museum piece. The birth of Christ is an interactive celebration, an ageless production that invites the miracle of incarnation into our homes at exactly the right time.

May this Advent be a season of matchless grace and abiding hope. The wise still seek him.

Prayer: Thank you so much, great God, for the refreshing belief of children. Grant us the faith and the insight to follow the star with such confidence and such hope. Amen.

DEEP INSIDE ME I CARRY A STAR

Walk while you have the light, so that the darkness may not overtake you. If you walk in the darkness, you do not know where you are going. While you have the light, believe in the light, so that you may become children of light.

—John 12:35-36

Today is the first Sunday of Advent. Churches around the world will take a moment to light the candle that represents *hope*. Hundreds of millions of people will share the experience of worship—hearts and minds focused on Jesus, one in spirit and united in trust and anticipation. Every assortment and flavor of church imaginable—the living, breathing, worshiping community of faith; this is the communion of the saints.

"And that," as my wife, Rebekah, often says, "gives me chilly bumps!"

TO TEACH IS TO LEARN

Several years ago, early in my teaching career, I enjoyed the rare privilege of working with severely emotionally disturbed (SED) and autistic children. My program was very much hands-on.

Of course, that was back when I still had the physical energy to teach everything from toilet training and shoe tying to language acquisition, reading, and math—all while simultaneously juggling large piles of, at times, senseless school-system paperwork.

The semester in question had not been easy. "Gary," an enormous sixteen-year-old, had recently broken two of my ribs; "Eric" had torched a counselor's prized Saab convertible (they burn surprisingly easily); "Andy" had put two staff members in the hospital in the space of ten minutes; and "Darrell," bless his heart—I still have a soft spot for him—had just thrown the class television through a large window.

I tried extra hard to work with some of the families who lived in desperate need. One afternoon I took a detour to a destitute neighborhood and delivered a large basket of seasonal goodies. "Mike's" parents typically were hostile and uncooperative, but I talked their mean-looking dogs into letting me through the gate before climbing carefully onto the rickety porch.

The doorbell didn't work, but I rapped hard on the front door, and it slowly opened. The sickening smell of decaying waste wafted onto the porch. I knocked again, but nobody came. The pungent darkness seemed to repel any light that tried to enter. I was unable to see beyond the first few feet, but I knew there were people at home because I could hear them moving around.

Eventually, after calling their names a few more times, I tired of the deafening silence. I left the hamper just inside the door, hollered "Merry Christmas," and walked away. Mike's mother quickly grabbed the loot and slammed the door shut before I had even made it all the way through the gate.

I drove slowly back into town, dejected and weary, wondering what difference—if any—I made in a world that knew so much of disappointment and pain.

Fortunately, I was on my way to fetch my children from their after-school program—Andrew and Naomi's positive energy always served as a good pick-me-up—and we stopped in at the grocery store for a few supplies. We were waiting in line, looking at one of the displays next to the cash register, when the season of Advent hope began to work on my heart with the power and intention of redemptive grace.

Right there, wedged in a stack of cards produced by a local charity, a bright splash of color caught my eye. It was a picture of a child wearing a zany Santa hat and looking intently at the star of Bethlehem.

I did a double take because I thought I recognized the artwork. It reminded me of a batch my class had submitted to a holiday-themed competition earlier in the fall. I'd forgotten all about it.

Sure enough, there inside I found the signature "Nathan." It was one of my fifth-grade students. But it was the poignant words, faithfully reproduced from his distinctive wobbly writing, that instantly sent hot tears cascading down my cheeks. How could I have skipped over them so easily before?

"Deep inside me," the deeply troubled child had written, "I carry a star. A light sometimes only I can see."

And there it was: deep and abiding hope. Love. Peace beyond my own understanding. Promise. Faithfulness. Joy to the world!

"What's the matter, Daddy?" my children wanted to know.

"Everything," I confessed, "and then nothing at all."

I shook my head. "Sometimes I don't understand why it is that Christmas makes me so happy."

And there is always hope.

Prayer: Heavenly Lord, we pray that this Advent season will enable our light to glow in such a fashion that the world will be more fully illuminated by the beauty and the generous hope of your perfect love. Amen.

The Assurance of Things Hoped For

> Now faith is the assurance of things hoped for, the conviction of things not seen. Indeed, by faith our ancestors received approval. By faith we understand that the worlds were prepared by the word of God, so that what is seen was made from things that are not visible.
>
> —Hebrews 11:1-3

One day I had to run into the convenience mart to grab a receipt for my gas because the fuel pumps were being uncooperative again. Buttons don't work, PIN numbers won't take. Half the time the machine charges me for a car wash I didn't order, and it never seems to have any paper loaded when I press "Print Receipt."

As I entered the store, a man my age was just leaving. He held a giant handful of lottery tickets. "Good luck," encouraged the clerk behind the counter. "Maybe this will be the Big One."

"Crossing my fingers," the man replied. "I sure hope so." And off he went.

Well, it took everything I had not to tap the confused man on the shoulder and give him a timely lesson in semantics laced with a hearty dose of seasonal gospel.

"You don't *hope* you win a lottery," I wanted to say. "Nobody *hopes* they win a fortune on lottery tickets. That's not it at all! People *wish* they could win a fortune. Hope is essentially a theological response, and there's no theology in the lottery. Hoping and wishing are two entirely different concepts."

Wishers dream their wishing dreams, they watch life go by, and they play the odds. Wishers believe in luck, but they don't possess any faith; they look for solid things at the end of trumped-up rainbows; they dream pipe dreams, and they are usually disappointed. Wishers say, "Beam me up, Scotty," and their dreams are edged with desperate longing. Wishers plan to marry their dream girl, but they never do anything about asking her out. They talk of a career, but they never go to school. Wishers believe what their children say about their homework and their grades; they swallow everything the late-night hucksters say on those cheesy infomercials; they look for diamonds inside boxes of Cracker Jack; and they say "this is the year" their favorite baseball team will "go all the way." Reality is seldom a factor; nor is believing.

People who hope read their Bible, and they pay attention to the promises.

People with hope, however, faithful people who know the goodness of God's grace firsthand, don't need to gamble or compromise their reason. They know. Those who hope sing hymns such as "I know that my Redeemer lives! What joy the blest assurance gives!" (Samuel Medley, 1738–1799). People who hope read their Bible, and they pay attention to the promises. Hopers plan on solid things based on real information; hopers have faith—"the assurance of things hoped for, the conviction of things not seen" (Heb. 11:1).

Hope is planning to marry that dream girl because you know she loves you deeply, and you're confident she's not dating someone else. Hope is counting on a career as an attorney in your final year of law school. Hope does not deceive.

Hope is a providential assurance, and providence is that blessed confluence of confidence where God's intention for our future intersects with our faithful response in grateful obedience to God's guiding word.

Nineteenth-century hymn writer Edward Mote (1797–1874) wrote the following: "My hope is built on nothing less than Jesus' blood and righteousness. . . . On Christ the solid rock I stand, all other ground is sinking sand." If we understand little else on our Advent journey toward Christmas, let's understand that.

There is nothing else that solid, and there is nothing else that real. Certainly not Santa; absolutely not "good fortune." Not great shopping, nor even a booming economy. With God, there is no need for any kind of wishing at all. Through Jesus Christ, we can have a hope that means something.

> Now faith is the assurance of things hoped for, the conviction of things not seen.—Hebrews 11:1

Prayer: Thank you, gracious God, for the evidence of your love that we experience through the Advent of Jesus. Help us to understand the penetrating focus of that love more completely, more personally, and with unfailing belief. Amen.

TUESDAY

A CHRISTMAS TREE ANGEL AND THE STORY OF REDEMPTION

I have said this to you, so that in me you may have peace. In the world you face persecution. But take courage; I have conquered the world!
—John 16:33

Have you ever found yourself reclining in your favorite armchair, a cup of coffee poised on your lap, staring at the Christmas tree in the corner and kind of wondering? I mean really, let's be honest, what exactly is it in the wacky world of interior decorating that makes an oversized dead shrub so compelling?

Think about it. It's a tree; what is it doing in the living room? And then we cover the unfortunate specimen with the most hodgepodge assortment of mismatched paper products, figurines, glass ornaments, party favors, and angels. We top it off with tacky colored lights and handmade strings of snack food. What's that all about?

We talk about our commitment to save the forests, and spend extra money to bring home a "live" Christmas tree. But then we cut it off at the knees, strap it to the wall, plug it into a light socket, and electrocute the poor thing. After a while, parts of the tree start to die and fall off all over the rug. By the second week of December, any open flame within fifty feet is likely to result in Tannenbaum Flambé. *Somebody* help me understand!

Yet somehow, standing there dressed in a kind of horticultural drag, our Christmas trees have become just about the most enduring symbol of the season for families all the way from London to New York to San Francisco.

In our house, the tree—or several trees, depending on my wife's decorating inclination—has become a visual journey into family history, an archaeological dig on a stick, evolving over the years into an elaborate seasonal scrapbook pasted together as events and people pass through our lives. Each ornament has its own story to tell, from first-grade handkerchief angels, to the handcrafted ornament purchased in Appalachia when we were expecting our first child, to the sterling-silver pinecone given by a generous friend who often shared our celebrations.

Our Christmas tree moves from everyday worldly images—such as trains, singing birds, and snowy houses—up through drummer boys, Santas, and nutcrackers—to a sacred host of stars, angels, and Nativity scenes toward the top. I remember when the children were little and Andrew, proud of his growing but inaccurate vocabulary, loudly informed a guest that our tree had "sacred ornaments at the top and sexual ones lower down"!

It is that meeting place of the sacred and the secular that makes the Christmas tree such a durable and endearing feature of our holiday homes.

It is that meeting place of the sacred and the secular that makes the Christmas tree such a durable and endearing feature of our holiday homes. Even the least religious feel compelled to stick an angel on its apex, include a Nativity scene underneath, or place a star near the top. Thus we give voice to the yearnings of all hungry hearts to undertake such a journey—as wise people still do today—following the star, making our way to public worship, singing carols, or at least pausing in some fashion to acknowledge the newborn King.

Our own angel was brought back from a mission trip to Haiti more than twenty years ago. She's a tattered homemade doll purchased on the dirty streets of Port-au-Prince and initially rejected as "too ugly to keep as a gift" by my niece. But eventually Miss Haiti found her way to adorning the very top of our Christmas tree.

"She represents what God means by Christmas," Rebekah explains each year. "Christ came for the poor, the rejected, the oppressed, and the dispossessed as much as he came for any of us."

So there our challenged angel sits every year, ugly yet beautiful at the same time. She decorates the top of our exceptionally gaudy tree, our wonderful symbol of hope and peace and redemption. She tells the most beautiful story of how Christ was born—she tells it unfailingly, and she can testify personally as to how the newborn King died for absolutely everyone. She will tell the truth about Advent so long as we have a tree for her to preach from, and, always, she will share the eternal story of hope.

Prayer: Creator of all life, Advent can transform people from darkness into light. We think of your goodness, we think about your love, and we understand that without you there is no durable hope in this world. Thank you for your amazing gift. Amen.

WEDNESDAY

THE PROMISE OF THE ANGEL CHOIR
THE ADVENT OF HOPE

But the angel said to them, "Do not be afraid; for see—I am bringing you
good news of great joy for all the people: to you is born this day in the
city of David a Savior, who is the Messiah, the Lord."

—Luke 2:10-11

L ots of excitement at Maul Hall," I e-mailed a friend in December.
"You can taste the anticipation around here. Our house is beginning to look and feel like an advertisement for hope."

At the same time I remember noting a considerable downtrend in the
amount of loot stashed under the tree. Several good reasons account for
the shift. First, at the time Scout the Labradoodle (my wife's then six-
month-old Labrador/standard poodle mix) was demonstrating an enthusiastic interest in any new item introduced to the environment. Wrapping
paper, tape, ribbon, ornaments, candles, wreaths, garlands, and fruitcake
were all considered fair game by the puppy. Even the long-suffering Magi
had made several unscheduled epic journeys. The odds of all three wise
dudes actually making it to Christmas Eve with their limbs intact or a
camel to ride on were fairly slim by the second week of December.

Then there's the question of need. I'm always the first to admit we
don't lack much around here. I already have a coffeemaker. We own a
wonderful twenty-eight-year-old stereo. The television works fine. I also
have decent golf clubs, thanks, even if they don't always work and sometimes hit sideways. We're discovering it makes a lot more sense to address
the needs of others instead of accumulating more stuff.

Plus there's economic reality; namely, our son's shiny new college degree and our daughter's amazing wedding. We cherish both celebrations with glad and overflowing hearts. The bottom line, however, remains: we have absolutely everything we could possibly want, so why feed the machine?

Finally, there is our deepening understanding of the consummate gift that is hope, a Christmas present God has already given. Passing this gift on to others always helps to put the season in perspective. Christ is life, and where there is life there is hope.

All this begs some obvious questions:

- Why even do Christmas? and hope "for what" or "in what" exactly?
- What's the point, if it's not about getting all the extra stuff?
- What remote relevance could our observance of a birth two thousand years ago possibly have to this world today?

The answers bring us right back to the phenomenal gift of good news as delivered by the angel choir. One huge Advent question we must consider is the implication of the angels' promise. The noisy mob frightened the stuffing out of a handful of shepherds on a quiet hillside; they had to have something significant in mind. "Glory to God in the highest heaven, and on earth peace among those whom he favors!" they trumpeted (Luke 2:14). Goodwill? Glory? Peace? Right here on earth? Now there's a Christmas present worth saving up for.

I'd like to invite each one of us to approach our observance of the holidays with the assurance of hope front and center. We can ask ourselves, *How can I pass forward such a gift in my home? How can I add a measure of hope to my relationships? How can I bring hope to my place of business? What might hope mean for my community? How might my life eloquently deliver this message throughout the world?*

The Christmas kind of hope is unrelated to any holiday-gift wish list. It is grounded in spiritual knowledge; it is revealed in the experience of grace; it is born in Jesus. Hope is proactive; it is action-oriented; it is unlike any empty wish. It has everything to do with the message of the angels and everything to do with the reality of the Cross.

The Christmas kind of hope confronts disappointment and emptiness head-on. It is not satisfied with platitudes. It deals entirely in the realm of reality. Christmas hope is built around a relationship with God that actually means something.

Hope doesn't settle for cheap wrapping paper, and it doesn't settle for second best. It is confidence and trust in the very best that God had to give us. That's exactly why the Messiah was born in the Bethlehem stable to begin with.

Here's a second invitation: take another look at Jesus. Let's surround ourselves with people who love God, and let's pay attention to the amazing story. Let's listen to the music with our hearts as well as our ears, and let's leave ourselves open, even if only just a crack.

Let's also be sure to participate in an Advent Communion service. The Lord's Table offers the one certain place where we can know and experience redemptive hope. Why? Because the bread and the wine represent the Cross, the radical commitment Christ offered from the very beginning to launch the initiative of a hope that actually stands for something solid. Hope that has staying power. Hope that is eternal and true.

Prayer: Thank you, God, for the impact your love has on all our lives. Thank you for the reality of hope found in both the stable and the Cross. Challenge us to respond with courage to the opportunities we find to give the gift of hope to this needy world. Amen.

THURSDAY

A FISH-EYE VIEW
OF PROMISE AND MERCY

Mary said,
"My soul magnifies the Lord,
    and my spirit rejoices in God my Savior,
for he has looked with favor on the lowliness of his servant. . . .
His mercy is for those who fear him
    from generation to generation."

—Luke 1:46-48, 50

Mealtime devotions are a wonderful vehicle for learning the truth about the character and the mercy of our God of hope. This principle holds, irrespective of how a family is defined: a single parent with one child, the "traditional" nuclear family, two sisters sharing a small apartment, an older sibling nurturing what's left of a broken home, a retired couple raising grandchildren, friends splitting rent to make ends meet, nontraditional households, or a complex interlocking family system spanning several busy generations.

However we add the numbers, the equation is always incomplete without deliberate family devotional time in the encouraging presence of Creator God.

One evening when our children were young, we were reading about God's mercy running "from generation to generation" (Luke 1:50). Prayers had included thankfulness to our God of hope, and also gratitude for the gift of family as a place where we can learn more about God's love. It was just a few weeks before Christmas.

After devotions the telephone rang. Andrew answered politely. "It's 'Mrs. Delightful,'" he told us. "But she doesn't want to talk to me." "Mrs. Delightful" was one of his teachers, and she wanted to speak with a parent.

The walk to the telephone in the kitchen seemed very long. I could almost feel the cold, hard bench outside the principal's office back in England when I was a child. I quickly questioned my son: "Is there anything you need to tell me before I pick up this phone?"

"No," he replied. Then he shrugged his shoulders. Somehow that gesture didn't make me feel any better.

It turned out Mrs. Delightful wanted "a conference." Actually, she wanted to talk with both my wife and me at the same time. And no, she said, it wasn't anything she could explain over the phone. But yes, it was very important.

Mercifully, both Rebekah and I were free at the same time the very next day. I was certain that my son's school career was over. So we prepared ourselves, nervously, fearing the worst, all the time prodding Andrew for clues. He continued to insist that he had no idea.

I arrived at the school the next day just a little over five minutes late. Rebekah was already in the classroom, and as I opened the door I could see that both she and Mrs. Delightful were smiling. My wife shoved some drawings into my hands; Andrew had been busy with his pencil and crayons. "Isn't this marvelous?" she said. "We've been looking at his creative work."

The particular piece of art that precipitated the conference was a fish-eye view of the bottom of a small boat. We could clearly make out fishing lines and floats bobbing in the water below the hull. One watery image of a man could be seen peering over the side directly into the field of view. A muted patch of yellow represented filtered sunlight. The instructions had been simple: "Children, I'd like you to draw a picture of a boat." Every other child in the class had sketched the perfunctory half-moon boat profile sitting on top of wavy lines that represented water. Mrs. Delightful had been exactly right; this wasn't something you could explain over the phone.

The three of us spent the next thirty minutes talking about how we might possibly channel the exciting creativity of a precocious, though admittedly rambunctious, hard-to-direct student. The conference was one of those unusually pleasant school-related parenting experiences, the ones you hold on to for the teen years when you're really going to need them.

Another school year found our son at a loose end in class because he consistently finished his assignments early. Many educators would have punished him for disobedience, for rushing his work, for roaming the room, and for leaving his desk without permission. Instead, his imaginative teacher put our high-energy offspring in charge of classroom research.

"You have to show me your work first," she cautioned, "and it has to be done carefully. But I know you enjoy looking things up, and you're always reading the encyclopedias. So, now you're in charge of research."

Once again, instead of despair we found hope in the very area where we were concerned. We gave thanks for Mrs. Delightful, and later for Andrew's teacher "Ms. Positive." Both conferences prompted us to give thanks to God—the God of creativity; the God who loves children and who made them all unique; the God who takes our sometimes confusing potential and molds it into God's good work. Immanuel, who entered this world in time and space because we are the children God loves.

Prayer: Thank you, Lord, for the constant of hope that you add to every aspect of our lives. Teach us to listen for your goodness and grace, and to communicate truth to the world every hope-filled day of our lives. Amen.

FRIDAY

HOPE THAT GROWS LEGS
AND WALKS IN THIS WORLD

And God said, "Let the earth bring forth living creatures of every kind:
cattle and creeping things and wild animals of the earth of every kind."
And it was so. God made the wild animals of the earth of every kind,
and the cattle of every kind, and everything that creeps upon the ground
of every kind. And God saw that it was good.

—Genesis 1:24-25

There's nothing quite like the day my church turns our average-
looking fellowship hall into a virtual barnyard. The occasion
typically comes along the first Wednesday of Advent: our quite
remarkable Alternative Holiday Gift Market, an evening of well-
managed chaos designed to raise money and deliver hope on behalf
of my favorite mission venture, Heifer International ("Ending Hunger;
Caring for the Earth").

Picture the senior pastor adorned in an inflatable pig suit, making hog-
calls and posing for pictures to attract attention to her booth. Or the chair
of finance floating around in a giant bee costume, while a herd of three-
year-olds dressed as water buffalo bellow at everyone they see.

Each ministry area takes on responsibility for a different animal, and
by the time the appointed day rolls around, the church has been transformed into a kind of "Barnum & Bailey meets Old MacDonald in a
crowded Moroccan bazaar" variety show.

Chickens. Rabbits. Heifers. Llamas. Goats. Pigs. Bees. Water buffalo.

Sheep. Chicks. Ducks. Geese. People can even buy trees. In the center of the mess, a team of steady hands inscribe gift cards in calligraphy, so friends and relatives all over the United States can receive Christmas greetings that include creative sentiments.

These are some of my favorites:

"Dear Great-Uncle Dan, this year an old goat was sent to a family in Honduras in your name!"

"Congratulations on another new baby. A trio of rabbits just arrived in Afghanistan in your honor."

"We know you like to pig out over the holidays, so we named two big fat hogs after you and sent them to rural Guatemala to help start a new industry."

The mission of Heifer International (www.heifer.org) is hope. Or, spelled another way, "to work with communities to end hunger and poverty, and to care for the earth." As one way to achieve this goal, Heifer places living animals in impoverished areas. Workers provide careful training in animal husbandry and Economics 101 to the recipients, along with the assurance of ongoing support.

The replenishment of hope is fundamental to Heifer's philosophy: hope in and through hardworking indigenous peoples who often just need a jump start. Consequently, most of the animals are pregnant the day they arrive, so the firstborn calf, piglet, rabbit, chick, etc., extends the chain of hope when passed on as a living gift to another family.

The fun for church and other advocacy groups comes in raising consciousness, purchasing real animals, and then knowing exactly where the critters are going. And when I say fun, I mean we have a blast! Hope, it turns out, is good for everyone involved.

The genius of our approach is friendly competition. Will the men's breakfast-group goats, for example, outdo the associate pastor and his llamas? Will the senior pastor's pigs outsell the mission team's rabbits? Will the youth's drive for bees raise more money than the worship ministry's campaign to plant trees?

A couple of years ago one of our elders asked the local Chick-fil-A manager to send a guy in a cow suit to add a little interest to his booth's promotion of the signature heifer. The folks at Chick-fil-A were so impressed with the spirit of rampant generosity that the next year they asked if they could cater a light supper. The restaurant sold more than 250 meals—then turned around and donated the proceeds to Heifer.

Hope is not only a lot of fun; hope is contagious.

After a few of these events, Heifer International's regional representative wanted to know how our little church could raise so much money. I guess the Heifer folks didn't truly understand the dynamic relationship between believing with joy and giving with abandon. The words of Jesus came to mind. "Come and see," we said. They did, and we quite simply blew them away.

"No one else in North America does it like this," the Heifer representative said halfway through the outrageous evening of organized confusion and constructive pandemonium. "The members of your church appear to be happy about writing big checks and forgoing traditional Christmas gifts," she said. "I didn't think there would be anything left over to give at this time of the year."

First off, we don't give from our leftovers; we have learned to give out of our firstfruits. Besides being fun and contagious, hope is plenty generous too. Interestingly, and in perfect response to detractors who argue that too many special offerings compromise the flow of funds to essential church operations, we have found a direct correlation between sacrificial giving (at events such as the Heifer Market) and increased pledges across the board to our general operating budget.

People who experience contagious fun in their generous response to hope find that they are full of belief as well. Hope is not only fun . . . and contagious . . . and generous; it turns out that hope also believes.

Prayer: Use us, loving God, as replenishers of hope. Grant us generous hearts through believing. Help us to understand that Advent prepares us for the coming of Jesus, and that the coming of the Christ is the advent of hope. Amen.

SATURDAY

KAIROS, THE RIGHT TIME FOR CHRISTMAS

In the beginning was the Word, and the Word was with God, and the Word was God. He was in the beginning with God. . . . From his fullness we have all received, grace upon grace.

—John 1:1-2, 16

There is something fundamentally unbalanced about the way we tend to run full tilt into Christmas every year. Headlong, like Advent is some kind of race; as if we have to get there first.

"Avoid the Christmas rush and shop now!" the advertisements say, and so we all rush to the mall the day after Thanksgiving, along with two million other people. Aerobic shopping, power retail, consumer meltdown. Then later we go hurtling back anyway, fired up to spend like so many lemmings, thirsty for more. "Only thirteen more shopping days till Christmas" has morphed into "Only thirteen days till Christmas" because now every single day is a shopping day—24/7 if we know where to look, and we certainly do. The meaning of the season seems dependent on our dexterity with a charge card.

Then, if the message is not clear enough already, we market Santa as some kind of prescient deity. We multiply our complicity when we blithely allow our children to believe their personal worth is measured by the number of presents the lord of Christmas deems they merit. "He's making a list, and checking it twice; Gonna find out who's naughty and nice. . . ." Santa Claus lives at the mall, and, faithful to the end, we leave our tithe at his shrine whenever we can find the parking.

One obsessive-compulsive newspaper writer once suggested we note all our seasonal goals on a superorganized Christmas checklist. We should systematize gift preparation in a "home wrapping center," she wrote, and implement production-line techniques in order to maximize efficiency.

Time is finite and there's only so much of it to go around, the market preaches, so if we don't utilize every single minute correctly, we will somehow be *under-Christmasized*. How *tragic*, I have been thinking. We wouldn't want that, now would we?

GOD'S TIME

Rebekah pointed out in church that the ancient Greeks drew on more than one word to understand the concept of time. *Chronos* describes time that is calculable, fleeting, consumable, and finite. Chronos is the kind of time that presses on us harshly, that so often leaves us both breathless and disappointed. The other word for time is *kairos*, the time of opportunity or of intervention. Kairos is the right time or the critical moment. Kairos is God's time, time that exists independent of such constraints as the rising and the setting of our sun in relation to this earth and our circumscribed terrestrial perspective.

> *Kairos is God's time, time that exists independent of such constraints as the rising and the setting of our sun in relation to this earth and our circumscribed terrestrial perspective.*

"Where did the time go?" is chronos time. "Only a few more shopping days left until Christmas," is chronos time.

"But when the fullness of time had come," Paul writes to the Galatian church, "God sent his Son" (Gal. 4:4). Our Savior was born at God's precise timing; in a very real sense Christmas is God's time for us.

We use the word *Advent* to help us understand the meaning of these often-hectic weeks leading up to Christmas. *Advent* means, quite literally, "a moving toward," and most of us have a great deal of moving forward to accomplish if we are going to be even a little prepared in kairos time for the coming of the Messiah.

Of course, we have the opportunity to move toward Christmas in either time frame—that is the beauty and the curse of our creation into freedom. Chronos or kairos? The true meaning of Advent, the only meaning of any real value, is found in kairos time: grace, encouragement, empowerment, Immanuel, hope. We miss the point of Advent entirely when we submit to the push and the press of chronos, compelling a season of frenetic and often ill-advised activity.

But we need not worry; there is plenty of time to accomplish what is truly important over these next few weeks. God created time for the ordering of our lives. And absolutely nothing in our chronos rush can possibly hold the power to frustrate our faith and our hope if we seek the infant Christ, struggling in the straw, born in Bethlehem, and offering the world his inestimable gift: the promise and the assurance of hope.

Prayer: Thank you, God of consummate hope and unlimited time, for your grace extended freely to our deepest needs, our most important hopes, and our most fervent prayers. Extend that gift to our needy hearts and fill our expectant souls. Our hope is in you, God. Amen.

WEEK 2

PEACE

INTRODUCTION TO PEACE

Enough Already with the Christmas Wars

The Spirit of the Lord is upon me,
because he has anointed me
to bring good news to the poor.
He has sent me to proclaim release to the captives
and recovery of sight to the blind,
to let the oppressed go free,
to proclaim the year of the Lord's favor.

—Luke 4:18-19

Category: Dates on the Church Calendar.
Answer—Daily Double: The source of our hope, the author of peace, and the only bona fide reason to celebrate Christmas Day.
Question: Who is Jesus?

Answer: The remarkable yet simple gift God gave the entire world, an infant born in a feed trough in a barn some two thousand years ago.
Question: Who is God's Son?

Okay, I'll admit that thousands of dollars in prizes and an invitation to come back as returning champion may not be riding on the correct answer. Nonetheless, a surprising number of us routinely enter this second week of preparation for Christmas with our initial trajectory so far off we're likely to miss the mark by a long shot. And that is some serious degree of jeopardy, so to speak.

We can get as politically correct as we like and bend over backward so as not to offend the sensibilities of nonbelievers. That's fine. But if—during this season of hope and peace—we allow ourselves for one moment to be distracted from the essential truth that leads to real peace, we might as well put away the decorations today. Because Christmas means absolutely nothing apart from Jesus.

Advent is about preparing our hearts for the coming of the Christ. Advent is all about gospel—the good news of Jesus. So it's going to be critically important to avoid distractions that cause us to lose track of the central message.

Case in point: the uniquely American Christmas Wars. You know, those petty skirmishes where Christians and nonbelievers fight around the dim lines of political correctness and argue about the constitutional relationship of church to state. There's still time to learn from our mistakes, so please, oh please, let's avoid unwrapping the same tired reactionary arguments this year. Instead, let's concentrate on the central message, the one the angels belted out with such gusto: "Glory to God in the highest heaven, and on earth peace among those whom he favors!" (Luke 2:14).

- Controversy over Nativity displays in public places.
- Store clerks forbidden to use the phrase "Merry Christmas."
- Store clerks required to use the phrase "Merry Christmas."
- The highly publicized removal, then much-ballyhooed return of Christmas trees in airport concourses.
- Nonsense spouted by American Civil Liberties Union spokespeople who are supposedly well educated and certainly should know better.

- Nonsense spouted by loud obnoxious Christians who claim to represent the Prince of Peace and who really should know better.
- Schools bullied into ignoring the Greatest Story Ever Told.
- Confrontation replacing the joyful celebration of "peace on earth."
- Politicians using "Merry Christmas" as their personal campaign slogan.
- Merchants who seem to believe the Holy Family were contracted to work directly with the folks over in Marketing.
- Merchants becoming nervous and giving the Holy Family a less-than-holy pink slip.

Wal-Mart—bless their corporate hearts—issued a statement in 2006 that offered the following glimpse into the politics of big business: "We're not afraid to use the term 'Merry Christmas,'" a spokesperson told *USA Today* that November. "We'll use it early, and we'll use it often." Consequently, many people took up the offensive. One organization, www.HelpSaveChristmas.org, prompted Americans to order an "Action Pak" designed to add a little clout to their angst. "Get two bumper stickers, two buttons, and both 'memos that helped save Christmas'—your complete Action Pak—*plus* help sponsor five church, school, or civic leaders to receive these powerful memos! Click here or see below. Receive one 'Help Save Christmas Action Pak' for any gift of $25 or more!"

I am a committed and very public Christian. I'm honest about my faith, and I let people know where I stand. My wife and I routinely embarrass our children by inviting strangers to church. Advent is all about Jesus and the wonder of his saving grace, and tens of thousands of people who read my newspaper column every week know precisely how I feel about the Prince of Peace. But, despite all that, I have zero tolerance for intolerance when it comes to climbing on the in-your-face-about-Christmas bandwagon. That's especially true when I think about exactly what it is so many misguided participants in the Christmas Wars are trying to save. Here's a partial list:

- Sectarian proselytizing disingenuously disguised as enthusiasm for Christ's message.

- Equal face time for the Prince of Peace, right up there with Rudolph, Frosty, Santa, MasterCard, Discovery, Visa, and the elves.
- The use of a displaced refugee family as a promotional tool for holiday shopping. (You have to admit, they do make compelling window dressing.)
- Garish reproductions of the Light of the world canned in tawdry illuminated plastic lawn ornaments.
- God's implied endorsement of conspicuous excess, personal greed, the abuse of consumer credit, and unrestrained consumption.

Why should we insist on playing the same tired game as everyone else? I believe the stand many Christians take actually makes Advent more confusing for nonbelievers. Why fight so hard to force faith into a common mold with the rest of society? Where is the peace in that? Why treat God as little more than one more interest group to mollify? Isn't Christianity supposed to be countercultural? Jesus certainly was.

We don't need a permit from city hall to accomplish the work of healing and grace or to live in truth and light. Jesus didn't come to shop. Christ came—how did he put it? "To preach good news to the poor . . . proclaim freedom for the prisoners and recovery of sight for the blind, to release the oppressed, to proclaim the year of the Lord's favor" (Luke 4:18-19, NIV).

I'm thinking maybe they can have Christmas, or at least *that* Christmas, the one we all seem to be so anxious about; I'm not so sure that we need it back. Maybe as Christians we should think seriously about enjoying that mythical line of separation between the secular and the sacred rather than struggling so hard to erase it, to pretend it isn't there, or to drag ourselves so completely into the mess that is the North American consumer culture that the gospel of truth ceases to have anything novel or revolutionary to say anymore.

Stick that in your stocking and put it under the tree.

This is a good time to huddle together with like-minded souls and make sure we are communicating the straight scoop about Christmas. That's a great goal for how we approach Advent. Peace is an action concept; it's not going to happen if we back away and let the darkness win. We cannot assume that the message is coming through clearly from anywhere else. Advent makes for a marvelous opportunity to share our faith, and it's critical that we begin this process by sharing the peace of Christ with our own family. In the sharing we probably will find our own faith reawakened—and our Advent illuminated—with both new hope and a deep, abiding peace.

The kind of peace you can take to the bank.

The kind of peace that is wrapped up in truth, and I'm talking about the kind of truth that works for healing and restoration.

It's the kind of peace that will lead us directly into the presence of Jesus.

Prayer: Reawaken our hearts to the witness of your love, Lord, and speak through our community of faith, our friends, and our families to a misinformed and confused world. We ask in the name of Jesus, who brings a peace that heals. Amen.

SECOND SUNDAY OF ADVENT

THE PRESENCE OF JESUS IN THIS WORLD

And you, child, will be called the prophet of the Most High;
for you will go before the Lord to prepare his ways,
to give knowledge of salvation to his people
by the forgiveness of their sins.
By the tender mercy of our God,
the dawn from on high will break upon us,
to give light to those who sit in darkness and in the shadow of death,
to guide our feet into the way of peace.

—Luke 1:76-79

John the Baptist's father, Zechariah, saw the Advent of the coming Christ as a clarion call to peace: Jesus as our guide; the tender mercies of God breaking open like the dawn; real light made evident where things had once been grim and dark. Forgiveness of sins would counter the shadow of ongoing defeat. What a vision, and what an inspiration!

But what on earth have we been doing here in this twenty-first century? What have we been up to, to demonstrate that we have chosen to follow Jesus? How do we participate actively in this vision and bring healing peace into the reality of our world?

A lot has been said about peace during this most turbulent past hundred years. There have been speeches, poetry, and folktales; countless hopes; beautiful dreams; and innumerable songs. But reality reveals a tragic contradiction. The more we talk about peace, the less tranquility and harmony we seem to actually witness.

THE HOME FRONT

My grandparents would tell stories about 1918, when millions of people stood in throngs on Armistice Day, both in London and around the world. It was a stirring sight, they said, and they cried passionately with all their hearts, "Never again!"

And they believed it. My grandmother Kemp's brother lied about his age, joining the British army at sixteen. He marched down to the docks with hundreds of other young men who also lied about their age, and he took the boat to Europe. Arthur Watts died in Belgium on Flanders Field, in the kind of wanton slaughter no one could bring themselves to believe the world would ever allow to happen again.

In my hometown of Folkestone, in the south of England, the hill the boys marched down on their way to the ships was later named the Road of Remembrance. But what did we all remember?

We remembered so poorly that, even though President Wilson won the Nobel Peace Prize for his efforts to establish the League of Nations in 1919, the U.S. government neither ratified the charter nor joined the organization. We remembered so poorly that the world went at it again, just two decades later. We killed one another off by the tens of millions. As Europe hurtled toward war in 1938, Britain's prime minister, Neville Chamberlain, signed the Munich Agreement. He desperately wanted things to be different, and he declared "peace in our time." But it was more like whistling in the dark, a move that virtually guaranteed a more devastating confrontation. He did not understand that real peace has nothing to do with fear.

GIVE PEACE A CHANCE

Unless we find a way to actively engage "the tender mercy of our God," and then make sure it really does break in like the dawn (Luke 1:78), our failed attempts at peace are always going to fall short and only be added to the list of hopeless clichés. In the 1960s, flower children stuck flowers in the barrels of National Guardsmen's guns; meanwhile, other young people died in the struggle for Vietnam.

Beatle John Lennon's haunting plea to "Give Peace a Chance" became the anthem of a generation, but he was murdered by a dark soul frantic for attention and in serious need of God's tender mercies.

Today some Christian pastors enthusiastically support war from their pulpits because they honestly believe it will hasten peace; while others protest any hostile action because they believe violence is always contrary to God's purposes.

Military veterans return home with missing limbs. Though mutilated and having witnessed horror, many believe passionately in the job they are doing. We all want to see the end of conflict. Good people with deep consciences openly disagree. But we all concur that the world needs to know a lasting and meaningful peace. Peace remains elusive and at best conditional and temporal in a world defined more and more by conflict and pain.

Peace remains elusive and at best conditional and temporal in a world defined more and more by conflict and pain.

BE THE PRESENCE OF JESUS

What are we really talking about, then, when we throw the word *peace* around so easily yet so earnestly? The dictionary defines peace most notably in the negative. It's a treaty to cease hostilities; it's the absence of mental stress or anxiety. Peace is harmonious relations; it's freedom from disputes; it's the prevailing state during the absence of war; it's the absence of armed conflict; or it's a kind of public quiet.

Most of us buy into this "absence of" model on a regular basis. Have you ever walked into your kitchen and announced, at the top of your lungs, "ALL I WANT AROUND HERE IS A LITTLE PEACE AND QUIET!!!"

Jesus is the Prince of Peace; we can find the antidote to our most common misconceptions in the person, the actions, and the message of Christ. His beautiful way challenges us to see peace not as a negative or neutral condition but as dynamic, purposeful, and vigorous.

The peace of God is not so much the absence of anything as it is the presence of so much. We can begin our weeklong emphasis on peace by inviting the tender mercies of our God to bring light into whatever darkness we find around us. We can be the presence of Jesus in this world. We can renew our commitment to God's way. We can make a difference.

Prayer: Gracious God, author of our lives, thank you for your active and purposeful love. Wash us with the refreshing waters of your peace. Use us to bring that peace to our world. Challenge us to serve you faithfully. Amen.

LOOKING FOR CHRISTMAS
IN ALL THE WRONG PLACES

And the Word became flesh and lived among us, and we have seen his glory, the glory as of a father's only son, full of grace and truth. . . . From his fullness we have all received, grace upon grace. The law indeed was given through Moses; grace and truth came through Jesus Christ.
—John 1:14, 16-17

Here in the town of Brandon, teetering on the eastern edge of Tampa's suburban sprawl, our much-beloved humongous shopping mall has just completed a 200,000-square-foot expansion as well as extensive renovations.

I find Christmas shopping in Florida a far cry from the gift-buying adventures I remember growing up in the wintry southeast of England. I thought nothing of hiking to the shops in foul weather, burdened by raingear and umbrella, and walking endlessly between the few choice stores that may or may not have offered the particular item I had in mind.

Today, in Tampa, people sport shorts, flip-flops, and T-shirts. Some stores offer valet parking. We complain if we have to walk more than twenty-five yards to an entrance. Our mall offers four coffee bars, conveniently spaced to ease our passage through the entire fleecing experience. We listen to our personal selections of seasonal music and enjoy air-conditioned, traffic-free access to an inconceivable range of ready merchandise. Then, like so many willing victims under group hypnosis, we charge extravagant items we can't nearly afford but somehow believe we need.

When I was a young adult, I paid only in cash and spent far less, yet somehow I felt more generous. Music was provided by Salvation Army musicians, huddled together under an awning to stay dry. Coffee was something exotic and incomprehensible.

One December, back when I was attending college in Florida, I experienced a crisis in Christmas faith. Just three days before Christmas, I suffered a near panic attack when it dawned on me that I had yet to experience even a morsel of a twinge of genuine seasonal peace. In a rush of homesickness, I blamed the palm trees and the green grass and Florida's warm nights for my spiritual vacuum. I fingered busy shopping plazas, Disney, climate-controlled malls, consumer excess, and American accents. I made myself believe that the only possible road to real Advent peace required a trip down memory lane into Christmas past. I knew with a delusional certainty that I had to board a plane, fly east, and return home in my noble Christmas quest.

Somehow I arranged a last-minute flight via Miami into London's Gatwick Airport. My parents met me there, more than happy to welcome me back into the fold.

NOSTALGIA

"I want to do it all," I announced. "I want to walk to the town center like I used to. I want to fight traffic and squeeze into impossible parking places. I want to jump up and down stomping my feet and clapping my hands because I'm cold and wet. I want to eat fish-and-chips out of yesterday's newspaper. And I want to sip scalding hot chocolate in that café upstairs at the Bobbies' Department Store where that glitzy guy in a white tuxedo plays requests on the grand piano."

It had been a long night of travel, I had not slept a wink, and I was breathless with excitement because I couldn't allow myself to understand that I felt so empty inside because I had forgotten about Jesus, the only authentic source of hope, peace, love, and joy I could really ever know. I wanted to believe that the familiar surroundings, the cold air, and the comforting feel of hometown holiday shopping would give me the seasonal fix I had thus far been unable to conjure.

Even today, thinking back, the idea almost makes sense. Don't we all go overboard sometimes in setting up the appropriate "atmosphere"? Aren't we disappointed when Christmas weather is too muggy, too wet, too warm? Don't we worry about getting the decorations just right and setting the traditional food out and singing the same Christmas songs that always make us sigh? And don't we want to curl up and cozy down with the melancholy and longing?

Isn't it difficult sometimes to distinguish the difference between hearts appropriately prepared to receive the King of kings, and that warm, fuzzy feeling we get when we've produced just the right balance of festivity and nostalgia?

REALITY

"Dear," my mother said patiently when I finished my wish list and finally came up for air. "That nice man stopped playing the piano years ago, when you were eleven years old." But it didn't matter. I knew with certainty that I'd find what I was looking for. So I looked up old friends and sampled tradition like the old hometown was some kind of nostalgia theme park.

Sometimes it takes a moment or more of desperation to achieve the kind of clarity necessary to hear God's voice.

My search came up empty; nothing seemed to work. Then on Christmas Eve, desperate now, I talked my brother into finding a church that offered a late candlelight service, and we quietly slipped in as the choir processed up the aisle. I'd flown all that way and spent pretty much every last penny I had. I was open to anything other than going to bed with the prospect of waking up Christmas morning still disappointed.

Sometimes it takes a moment or more of desperation to achieve the kind of clarity necessary to hear God's voice. I felt completely empty, and that—I believe—is what finally tipped the balance, an emptying of all that

I am and all that I can control. The congregation joined to sing "In the Bleak Midwinter":

What can I give him, poor as I am?
If I were a shepherd, I would bring a lamb;
if I were a Wise Man, I would do my part;
Yet what I can I give him: give my heart.*

It finally hit me. I felt relieved and forgiven and free, and I think I cried again, only this time in thanksgiving, this time in receiving the peace of Christ. Peace that is beyond my comprehension, and almost always just beyond my reach.

Advent in a busy shopping mall or Christmas in a cold English town square? Preparation at home with my parents or in the hallowed mystery of late-night Episcopalian Communion? What about muggy Florida? There, or anywhere at all, Christmas must be about grace and peace. Peace—God's peace—extended lovingly and freely to the point of my deepest need, my most important hopes, and my most fervent prayers.

Prayer: Gracious God, please extend your gift of peace to our needy and confused lives. Grant not just a seasonal but a soulful knowledge of your abiding peace. Amen.

* Christina G. Rossetti (1830–1894)

WE WISH YOU AN INSTANT CHRISTMAS AND A FREEZE-DRIED NEW YEAR

"Though the mountains be shaken
and the hills be removed,
yet my unfailing love for you will not be shaken
nor my covenant of peace be removed,"
says the LORD, who has compassion on you.

—Isaiah 54:10, NIV

One of my work friends asked what I enjoy most about Christmas. I immediately answered, "The preparation." What I meant, of course, was "Advent."

Sometime Christmas morning, but not too early, Rebekah will finally open my gift to her, an event I have been planning and anticipating for literally weeks now; the moment will be magical—it always is. I know I'm going to enjoy that split second of emotion; giving always brings me joy, and such consummation of expectation is a real rush. But it is in the getting there—the planning and the choosing and the wrapping and the suspense—that I find the deepest levels of meaning.

The Christmas Eve candlelight service at my church embodies much the same dynamic. This undeniably beautiful occasion is probably my favorite worship experience of the year, but for me the most enduring measure of Advent peace is always revealed in the journey. The days and weeks leading up to Christmas are like a huge cauldron where the Advent season simmers in graduated expectancy. Each added experience becomes one more key ingredient adding to the flavor, especially when prepared by hand and stirred in with love.

I fail to understand why so many people profess to find satisfaction in taking shortcuts that dilute the experience or—worse—eliminate the mystery altogether. "We yanked the tree out of the box and then plugged it right into the wall," I heard a man announce one day. "That sucker was predecorated with colored lights and a bunch of ornaments. It took three minutes tops. None of this three hours and listen to Christmas music nonsense for me!"

Not to be outdone, his friend bragged how he avoided the pain of thoughtful shopping. "Fifteen gift cards from the same Web site," he boasted. "Three clicks of the mouse and a credit card number. In and out; five minutes and I'm done."

Great, I thought. *Congratulations. Maybe we can compress Advent into one week while we're at it and then Easter into a convenient afternoon. That way we can minimize the distraction from the compelling routine of normal life.*

Each ornament on our tree represents something unique. The bumble-bee angel the children made, the stained-glass bell lovingly crafted by an old friend, the treasured cornhusk seraph we found in Appalachia the week we discovered we were expecting our first child, the doll Rebekah brought back from Haiti that gently reminds us Christ came for everyone.

Advent is process, process that comes loaded with peace a layer at a time. We can't assemble our Christmas without engaging memories, tears, laughter, joy, and penetrating meaning. We wouldn't hang lights from our rooftop if we weren't prepared to consider the message we illuminate. We don't put a wreath on our door or a manger scene on the table without retelling the ancient story of hope and of joy and of peace.

Why drag a tree into the living room if we're more concerned with getting back to the game or watching the show? Why bother buying gifts if we're not prepared to invest time and love in the process? Why shortchange ourselves when we could be enjoying an Advent that might change our lives? Why shortchange God?

Maybe too many of us are afraid of real change. Maybe we don't want any more than the CliffsNotes version of Christmas. Maybe we need a John-the-Baptist kind of message to jolt us into being ready for the coming Christ. Maybe our feet need to be guided into his challenging way of peace.

"The rising sun will come to us from heaven," John the Baptist's father said, "to shine on those living in darkness and in the shadow of death, to guide our feet into the path of peace" (Luke 1:78-79, NIV). The path of Advent peace doesn't interface well with instant, prepackaged, superconvenient, or freeze-dried. The path of peace is a real and often challenging journey. The path of peace goes directly through Bethlehem . . . and then it continues—without hesitation—to Jerusalem and the Cross.

Prayer: Thank you for your reassurance that the path of peace does not end at Calvary, Lord, and that we need not take such a journey alone. Strengthen our witness, we pray, so that grace and peace will be evident in the way we live your truth. Help us to find the right meaning in all the traditions we enjoy so much. Amen.

WEDNESDAY

UNDERSTANDING WHAT GOD IS UP TO

Peace I leave with you; my peace I give to you. I do not give to you as the world gives. Do not let your hearts be troubled, and do not let them be afraid.

—John 14:27

If this "Christ peace" we are talking about really is an active con-struct—rather than merely something passive or quiet—then how, exactly, do we *do* peace? If peace is much more than being unbothered or left alone, then what exactly is it? If people are happily experienc-ing the dictionary definition (absence of conflict), then what must we understand to know genuine peace on a spiritual level?

The answer is "Advent." This is where the practice of peace comes into its own. When we need an explanation for the meaning of peace, we can begin with the promise of Jesus. Peace took residence on earth in the birth of Christ. God redefined peace and presented the world with a flesh-and-blood working model of his new explanation. God designed Christmas to shake up the full created order. It offers those of us follow-ing Jesus today a new and deeper understanding of a worn concept.

In the bustle of an overcrowded market town at the height of tax sea-son; in the noisy courtyard of a busy inn, shuffled without dignity amid the braying donkeys and other restless animals; in the middle of oppres-sion, darkness, displacement, and poverty, there was peace. It was there, into the hub of tension and confusion, that God sent the Prince of Peace. It was there, in the middle of real life, that God made flesh his intention to change our way of thinking.

The tired parents and the cranky newborn Jesus were doubtless exhausted; maybe the small family was even getting a little early-morning shut-eye. Suddenly, a crowd of wide-eyed shepherds busts in. And they're yelling: "You all will never believe what we just saw up in the hills!"

What an unwelcome interruption! Yet peace, clear and overwhelming, filled the hearts and the minds of all who were there that night, and they understood. They understood what God was up to and they knew. They knew peace, active and convincing. Peace, nothing whatsoever to do with the absence of anything. It was God's way, once again, of confounding the world.

Today, in this twenty-first century, our homes are readying for Christmas:

- The ornaments on the tree are placed with a perfect sense of balance.
- Each character in the manger scene occupies its appropriate position.
- The host of angels gathered together over the piano hover, just so.
- The wreath on the door is a vision in decorative greenery.
- The presents beginning to appear under and around the tree could have been wrapped and placed by Martha Stewart herself.

Let's face it, the children are grown up and they're pretty much, mostly, kind of, almost gone now. The place looks far too good. Our traditional "Gather around, everyone, and let's throw a bunch of ornaments on the tree until the box is empty" decorating technique typically left the family room looking like a category-five hurricane had just come through. But this year Rebekah and I took well over three hours. We listened to the Kenny G Christmas CD and sipped hot tea, taking our time.

It all certainly looks better, granted, but you know, something's just not right. In holidays past, setting out the manger scene qualified as a minidrama. "He had the baby Jesus last year." "Her camels are all bigger than mine." "I can't believe you put a plastic army guy in with the shepherds." We ended up letting the children alternate days, so they could each rearrange the tableau. Yet there was still sabotage: "One of my shepherds is hanging upside down from the ceiling fan. If he keeps going round and round like that, he's going to puke!" Kidnappings took place, and ransom notes appeared: "If Mary ever wants to see Joseph again, she needs to stand back behind the manger where I put her yesterday and promise not to ride the camel." And then there was bribery: "I'll share my cookie with you if you let Joseph hold the rocket launcher the rest of the week."

Nowadays our cat takes up the slack as best he can. He upends the occasional wise man, ambushes sheep who wander from the safety of the manger, and savages the odd ornament that dares to move in his presence. But Darth is mellowing in his middle years. Consequently, most of the meddling must be pursued by our new puppy, and I've got to admit, Scout the Labradoodle is doing her part.

But I miss the children. I miss them every day, but I miss them so much more at this time of year. I miss the front door slamming, followed by the pause while someone picks up what is left of the wreath. I miss Andrew's "Do I still have to wrap this if I can cram it into some kind of a bag?" I miss Naomi's constant need to shop. I miss their excitement in giving with such generous hearts.

Andrew plans to fly home the day before Christmas; Naomi and her husband probably will spend the night with us on Christmas Eve. Together we'll all attend the candlelight service at church. But this year my prayer is simple, and the gift I crave sublime: I want both children and Naomi's husband, Craig, to cherish our family. I want them to appreciate the amazing privileges we enjoy, the blessings of our loving home, and the freedom to worship without fear. But, more than that, I want them to know peace, deep-down and abiding. I want our children to experience home in the most profound sense that the season can offer. I want them to hold their candles on Christmas Eve, burning brightly in steady hands, and I pray from the bottom of my heart that they all understand the meaning of such light, that they fall on their knees, and that they know beyond a shadow of a doubt the Savior, Jesus, who is their hearts' true home.

Because, in truth and in joy, in abiding peace, Christmas will have come once again.

Prayer: All-seeing God, we are aware that your radical perspective often differs from ours and constantly challenges us. We pray for the courage to allow our lives to be influenced by your way—"peace not as the world gives"—peace beyond human understanding. Amen.

THURSDAY

PEACE IN A NOISY HOUSE

The LORD bless you and keep you; the LORD make his face to shine upon you, and be gracious to you; the LORD lift up his countenance upon you, and give you peace.

—Numbers 6:24-26

I'm guessing the occupants of Maul Hall are not the only family members who live in a sometimes noisy house. Advent, Christmas, summer, or spring; you name it; there's going to be the occasional decibel or so floating around.

I'm not talking about TV noise or the stereo, and it's not anything like yelling—that's the last thing you're going to hear around here. It's just that the house can be noisy: the telephone; one or more of those pesky cell phones; the dog; the dog doing something to the cat; someone running machinery—a lot of the time, living is just noisy.

I remember cooking supper when the kids were little. The microwave does not defrost quietly; the exhaust fan over the stove is churning away (probably some Legos or something bouncing around in the mechanism); the "extra-low-noise" dishwasher is chug-chugging—we paid more for the "quiet" feature; and both the clothes washer and the dryer are humming along (most likely with the help of a sneaker or two banging around). In the living room, Naomi and some loud pop diva practice their radio sing-along—neither one holding anything back; Andrew is doubtlessly playing a computer game at top volume—educational, he always insists. Then Rebekah arrives home from work, the dog barks, and the decibels increase as everyone excitedly starts to talk at once. . . .

What a bustle. Our house is at peace. "Peace?" you say. Yes, absolutely. Because of the love that binds us together, the belief that inspires us, the commitment that adds substance to the trust, and the grace that works through community. All these find their genesis and their nourishment in the person of Jesus: Wonderful Counselor, Mighty God, Everlasting Father, Prince of Peace.

THANKSGIVING

It's exactly the same quality I stumbled across this past Thanksgiving. Somehow the fates have aligned to make our house the gathering place for both families. I haul in trestle tables from the church, and we rearrange enough furniture to seat twenty-some people around one long table.

The nieces and nephews help our young adult children dig out every piece of fine china and crystal in the house, and together they prepare a table that sparkles. Meanwhile, in the kitchen, we do what it takes to put together the feast. But it's later, after the long noisy banquet, that I typically resonate with seasonal peace. I'm in the kitchen, usually cleaning up solo because it's simpler to deal systematically with the mountain of party debris that way; and then I sometimes stop and listen.

What I hear is remarkably peaceful in an alternate-reality way. Loud children chasing one another around the garden; various groupings of animated conversation breaking out around the house; the clunk and tinkle of crockery as dishes are stacked; yells of delight as one more piece fits into the big puzzle we usually have going; Rebekah's brother Jesse playing the guitar; the rambunctious dog gently scolded for the umpteenth time for some ongoing breach of etiquette; Joe telling those lame but classic jokes nobody wants to miss; the younger nieces laughing their way through Rebekah's latest craft project on the porch; and of course the kettle boiling for tea.

All the while, I fall into the occasional circle of conversation since the kitchen opens out to the family room, and I'm not really alone. The place is literally ringing with clamor. A couple of older family members simply listen and smile, because it's almost too loud to talk, and certainly too jumbled for them to hear. Our home is packed solid with people, with festivity, with thanks, and with bedlam levels of noise.

Peace, healing peace, thankful peace.

If I ever get to be on the list of important people who decide stuff, I'm going to recommend a fifth week at the beginning of Advent. I'm going to call it "Thanks." Hope, Peace, Love, and Joy are important, but the whole thing will kick off in the context of Thanks.

My theology of peace is rooted in thanks. I know one thing for sure: when I'm up to my eyeballs in dirty dishes and leftover turkey parts, and when I look through my house to witness the collective noise of twenty-some family and friends enjoying boisterous communion in the name of gratitude, then I feel my heart burst in a kind of deeply peaceful thanksgiving. It could well be the perfect prelude to Advent.

Prayer: You are always so willing to teach us, Lord. Be with us this Advent, and teach us the meaning of peace. Teach us new things and in new ways, so that our experience and our understanding will grow in the ways that you intend. Introduce us to some children if it will help! We are so grateful for your patience and for your nurturing love, Lord. Amen.

FRIDAY

WOULD YOU LIKE SOME PEACE WITH THAT TRADITION?

And let the peace of Christ rule in your hearts, to which indeed you were called in the one body. And be thankful. Let the word of Christ dwell in you richly.

—Colossians 3:15-16

Tradition can be great, but once in a while, if we're not careful, it gets the upper hand. I grew up in England, so a December seldom passes without people quizzing me about the most obscure British traditions—some of which I have never even heard of! I do enjoy, however, talking about Father Christmas, plum pudding, Boxing Day, church on Christmas morning, the Queen's speech, and other happenings peculiar to an English yuletide.

I've even been known to make things up. You know, at the kind of social gatherings where no one knows anyone, and everyone makes small talk. "Yes, back in the 1970s I was invited to the lord mayor's traditional Yule Cake Ceremony. Women from all over England create Yule cakes using local ingredients. That's where I learned about Oxford udder pie and sheep-brain fruitcake from Yorkshire. Fortunately, I grew up in Kent." Truly meaningful to me, though, and very close to my heart, are the little things my family did that were peculiar to our home and our experience. It doesn't matter how British my family was, or how American you are, or Mexican or German or Peruvian, for that matter. What counts are the traditions that mean something, the practices that represent the essence of Christmas and teach us something new about God's great gift.

When I was growing up, for example, we stored presents in our rooms rather than putting them under the tree. Santa got credit only for the gifts in our stockings. On Christmas morning, every member of the family had a designated chair in the living room, and over the course of a half hour, each space would fill up as the gifts made their way downstairs. We opened our presents in turn, one at a time, as we went around the room. The small family Rebekah and I started has been together almost three decades. Early on we noticed we were blending traditions: something from my family, something from Rebekah's. The ones that stuck are the ones that resonate with the good news of Jesus.

I'll never forget the first Christmas my parents came to stay. I heard crying in the hallway, and I saw my mother standing there with a bulging stocking in her hand. "I haven't opened a stocking since I was thirteen," she sobbed. "Welcome home, Mum," I replied.

NEW TRADITIONS

One Christmas when the children were very young, we answered an ad from the Happy Christmas Tree Farm. The trip to the farm was a nightmare of whining, complaining, and fighting. The experience cutting the tree was worse. Then the drive back involved no fewer than three incidents of "We're pulling over to the side of the road, and we're not going anywhere until you stop fighting." We skipped our dinner treat; the tree fell off the roof twice; and by the time we made it home, I was ready to use the thing for firewood.

"That's the last time we go anywhere to cut our own tree," Rebekah said. I wholeheartedly agreed.

The next year I intercepted the Happy Christmas Tree Farm flyer and dropped it in the trash. I must not have buried it deep enough, because the children brought it with them to supper that night.

"You lost our invitation," Andrew said with a look of anticipation all over his nine-year-old face. Rebekah and I did a double take. "I thought we'd support the Boy Scouts and pick up a tree at the ball field," I offered.

"We can't do that, Daddy," Naomi chimed in. Andrew nodded in agreement. Little matter that we'd only ever gone to the "Happy" place once, and little matter the experience was an unqualified disaster. The children sealed our fate with a time-honored appeal: "But we *always* go to the Happy Christmas Tree Farm," they said in unison. "It's our family tradition."

The traditions we have developed over the years belong to us. They're not British, they're not American, but they are "Derek, Rebekah, Andrew, Naomi, Craig, and God" ones. That's my family; that's my experience of Christmas. And it's an experience cradled securely in the context of God's overwhelming love. It's a basis for tradition that I am proud and happy to share.

Honoring our faith traditions is a must if we are to know Christmas peace of any substance. If we don't have faith traditions deep in our experience, then it's incumbent on us to add them. Otherwise, our practices will be those pushed on us by the world of commerce, and that's not a message designed to bring us any closer to God. The healing and the creative force of God's tradition was born that day in the city of David. If we give ourselves back to God, and if we make it part of our tradition, then the rest of our celebration will reflect that grace. Christ is more than a good example; Christ is the way, the truth, and the life of our Advent celebration.

This Christmas, if we are indeed planning to follow God's way, then Jesus must be our Lord. Then we will also know his peace.

Prayer: Heavenly Lord, patient God, we ask today that you help us as we seek to rediscover what it is that we really celebrate every Christmas. Be the substance of our new traditions, and guide us into the path of peace. Amen.

SATURDAY

BE A JESUS-FOLLOWER AND LEAD THE WORLD INTO PEACE

For a child has been born for us,
a son given to us;
authority rests upon his shoulders;
and he is named
Wonderful Counselor, Mighty God,
Everlasting Father, Prince of Peace.

—Isaiah 9:6

All this is from God, who reconciled us to himself through Christ, and has given us the ministry of reconciliation; that is, in Christ God was reconciling the world to himself, not counting their trespasses against them.

—2 Corinthians 5:18-19

Recently I flew to another city in support of my first book, *Get Real: A Spiritual Journey for Men*. The plane was crowded, and just before we rolled away from the gate, an off-duty pilot squeezed into the seat next to mine.

We politely exchanged greetings and settled down for the flight. I pulled out my book, opened a legal pad, and started making notes for my presentation the next day.

"What are you reading?" the pilot asked, drawn in by the cool-looking cover.

"My own book, actually," I answered. "I'm teaching a group of men over the weekend."

"What's it about?" he inquired.

"It addresses the question 'What exactly does it mean to be a Christian man in the twenty-first century?'" I said. "There seems to be a lot of confusion on the subject, and I've tried to lay out a simple path."

"I've been meaning to take some steps closer to God for some time now," the pilot replied. "My life's turned into a real mess; I'd like to read your book."

We chatted for a few minutes, then one of the flight attendants said the captain had invited my new friend into the cockpit for the remainder of the flight. So I prayed for him and got back to my work.

Not long afterward, the plane landed, and close to two hundred tightly packed people squeezed their way out to the Jetway. As I approached the door, a hand reached through the crowd and grabbed mine.

"Thanks so much for talking with me," the hitchhiking pilot said. "Would you give me your card? I want to hear more about Jesus."

GENESIS

For me everything else that makes sense finds its genesis in the context of Christmas. The world, dark and distressed, suddenly infused with light in response to the coming of Christ. It's a reality that plays out in one form or another every year.

Virginia's classic question, "Is there a Santa Claus?" could easily be translated in this twenty-first century to: "Is there any hope at all anymore?" "Can we find some encouragement from anything or anybody?" "My life's a mess, and I'm looking for some peace." Or, "Is there a Prince of Peace?"

Peace is pretty much our primary job as Christians; God has charged us with a ministry of reconciliation, of bringing the world and God's truth together, of reunion, and of resolution. That's why I get so frustrated when a so-called Christian witness turns people off instead of inviting them in. We live in a culture where the word *Christian* has picked up so many negative connotations that I've found myself substituting the term *Christ-follower* or *Jesus-follower* instead.

The Advent of Christ introduced the world to the possibility of real peace. We do not achieve reconciliation when we alienate the world; we achieve reconciliation by finding common ground, common purpose, and experiencing common joy.

I work as a freelance writer, and I can attest to the fact that the media industry loves negative stories about religion. Scandal, abuse, misappropriation, criminal behavior, and sexual deviance all quickly find their way to the front pages. If a church wants publicity, all it has to do is act contrary to the gospel. Infighting? Schism? Condemnation? Embezzlement? Perversion? It'll be on the evening news and all over the papers the next day. That's why I feel so privileged to be able to dialogue with tens of thousands of people via my newspaper column. It's my opportunity to tell the truth and to set the record straight. Interestingly, good news is well received; people enjoy reading about hope, peace, love, and joy.

The late Fred Rogers put it well in an interview on Arsenio Hall's late-night talk show (January 6, 1993). "It would be easier to believe," Arsenio said, "if God still did big impressive things. You know, like the Old Testament miracles." Rogers, a Presbyterian minister, quickly replied, "God's revealing evidence is everywhere; we just have to receive it." And that is where we find the Prince of Peace. His revealing evidence is everywhere. We just have to open our eyes.

Prayer: Lord, make me an instrument of your peace. Help me to be a compelling witness to the truth that the Prince of Peace is active in this world. Use me as a part of your revealing evidence, everywhere I go and through all that I am. Amen.

WEEK 3

LOVE

LOVE, THE PREFACE

Love Is the Story of Christmas

As God's chosen ones, holy and beloved, clothe yourselves with compassion, kindness, humility, meekness, and patience. Bear with one another and, if anyone has a complaint against another, forgive each other; just as the Lord has forgiven you, so you also must forgive. Above all, clothe yourselves with love, which binds everything together in perfect harmony.

—Colossians 3:12-14

Compared to many, my journey in this world has been fairly easy. Too easy, according to some. Members of a writer's group once lectured me, "You'll never be a real author until you experience some authentic pain in your life!" Well, I'm not one to play "Top your story" or "I've got bigger and better battle wounds," but Rebekah and I raised two children. We have known more than a little genuine ache in the heart. More to the point, and more apropos to this particular chapter, is the corollary truth: We have known far more than a little love as well.

Indeed, love *is* the story of Christmas, and the amazing story of Christmas introduces a new kind of love. In truth, agape love (in its deepest ramifications) was not even a shadow of the vaguest possibility before Christ. Love truly was born at Christmas.

CREATIVE LOVE

The power of love is the same power that creates; in fact, it is the only power that creates. Evil can only tear down and destroy, but love builds. I believe that—more than anything else—love is the necessary component of the creative process, especially if we intend to reflect the image of God. Love is the agent that introduces actual substantive change; it's the crucial element.

God is Love. God is the Creator. God created out of love, and God loves that which God created. We are made, the Bible tells us, in God's image. "So God created humankind in his image, in the image of God he created them; male and female he created them" (Gen. 1:27). If we are in any way to honor the image of God, then it is necessary that we love, and we must love creatively. We must create, and we must create lovingly.

> *If we are in any way to honor the image of God, then it is necessary that we love, and we must love creatively.*

It may be a truism to say that love is the universal language; to say, "All we need is love," or "Love makes the world go round." But such statements become clichés only because they are so true. Let's not dismiss truth because it is expressed in the form of cliché. Instead, let's do our best to express truth more creatively and to express truth with more love.

When I first dated my wife, Rebekah, I wrote songs for her because music was the closest I could come to expressing my feelings. I was a decent guitar player, and the words always flowed; I'm confident that my songs achieved something in their own way. Later, when we had children,

I realized how inadequate my music had been in comparison to creativity of the first order. Andrew and then Naomi were and are the most profound expressions of creative love I have ever imagined.

Of course I did not bring our children home like a bunch of flowers, or design them in my workshop. Nonetheless, because of my participation in God's creative love, in a way I guess that I did. Or at least in the same way that God and I collaborate in my music and in my writing. It's not so much that sex is love as it is that creation is love. Andrew and Naomi are a collaborative masterpiece of God's creative love in the context of my particular family. They are especially beautiful because my commitment to God, with Rebekah, was and is fundamental to our experience together.

YES, WE'RE TALKING ABOUT CHRISTMAS!

Here is where love amounts to all the substance of authentic Christmas, everything about Advent and celebration wrapped up together. Love—in flesh and blood and hope and promise—is exactly where God wants to meet us, and how God wants to meet us during this Advent season. *God desires fellowship with his children; God loved, conceived of, and created us, not for isolation but for relationship.*

God then made a brilliant and extravagant decision to place a new creation into this world—an entirely innovative expression of the divine love. Jesus comprises the same substance as the father (the Greek word, used in the Nicene Creed of 325, is *homoousia*). Jesus is creation all wrapped up in love, placed with such tenderness in the young girl Mary's womb, and then left to the devices of this evil world.

This is love beyond reason. As time goes by I have been more able to understand the impact of love on the promise of Christmas. More so as I have often felt my children slip through my fingers and beyond my immediate protection—from the minimal ten seconds or so our daughter, Naomi, hid behind a partition at the mall when she was three, to the multiple hours she was lost as a twelve-year-old, which involved two helicopters, three police dogs, and a prayer-chain as wide as our church family. What God must have felt, handing Christ off to Mary and Joseph, effectively gifting his only Son into this present darkness. . . .

Once, the day I thwarted a kidnapping attempt from Naomi's day care, I saw my child literally resting in the hands of evil. She was just fourteen months of age. My daughter was in a stranger's arms, and they were on their way out the door when I arrived. Only later did I realize the extent of what might have been and how profoundly thankful I was that I was able to save her.

LOVE HURTS

Love can hurt so deeply: the surgery, the night search, the car wreck, the trouble, the shattered dreams, and the broken heart.

The day Craig asked our daughter to marry him, I cried again. Then our son, Andrew, graduated from college and moved a thousand miles away. His car was packed, and he planned to leave right after church. I'd been playing guitar and was stuck standing at the front of the sanctuary when the choir led the congregational benediction, singing "Go now in peace. . . ." The song by Don Besig and Nancy Price affirms the certainty of God's constant love and care. I tried my best not to cry, but I felt hot tears streaming down my face as I joined in the words. Naomi saw me, walked to the front of the congregation, and put her arm through mine. Of course I cried even more.

So there I was, understanding love as profoundly as a father can, feeling some of God's intention in sending the promise of Jesus, wondering if I could even imagine God's pain in the decision. But yes, I can imagine; I can imagine on a level that brings more tears just in the thinking. And that's why I can write about it here, and that's why I am glad, so very glad, that Jesus came—for me, for Rebekah, for Andrew and Naomi, and for Craig. Jesus came for love. Love came for us all.

Prayer: Love lifts us up, God, and the kind of love that you introduced into the world that night in Bethlehem reaches deep and far into all our experiences this Advent. It is a love that was completed at Calvary, completed yet also just begun. Help us in our commitments to be worthy of such profound sacrifice and grace. Amen.

THIRD SUNDAY OF ADVENT

LOVE NEVER FAILS

Love is patient, love is kind. It does not envy, it does not boast, it is not proud. It is not rude, it is not self-seeking, it is not easily angered, it keeps no record of wrongs. Love does not delight in evil but rejoices with the truth. It always protects, always trusts, always hopes, always perseveres. Love never fails.

—1 Corinthians 13:4-8, NIV

Love came down at Christmas,
Love all lovely, Love divine;
Love was born at Christmas;
star and angels gave the sign.
—Christina G. Rossetti, 1830–1894

LOVE CAME DOWN AT CHRISTMAS

We often have a hard time with our language when it comes to describing the actions of God in a world limited by the constraints of time and space. *Down* doesn't exactly pinpoint the direction God's initiative moved that dazzling night in Bethlehem; neither is it the most descriptive. But, then, "Love infused the world with God's purpose and worked the dynamic intention of promise into the very DNA of creation at Christmas . . ." just doesn't fit very well with the music.

Usually by late December I have been well infused with love. And not just at church; I receive a lot of love's meaning from the collective goodwill many people show this time of the year. People tend to lower the emotional guard they wear so closely the other eleven months. Even when they don't get the essential message of Advent and Christmas, the vast majority do seem to allow themselves the indulgence of at least a little positive seasonal glow. For my part, I really do blame love. Love gets loose from its somewhat stuffy confines during Advent, and I for one couldn't be happier.

LOVE ALL LOVELY, LOVE DIVINE

There's nothing like generosity to release the meaning of love, and I know story after story of sad people who are changed to the very core when giving releases their passion. The way of love and of sacrifice potentially can enrich our Advent celebration with meaning unimaginable outside the context of a generosity that actually costs something.

When I was teaching in Atlanta I met "Sonya Brown," the first student to steal my heart. Sonya pulled me into the world beyond regular education and into classrooms inhabited by children who need more than reading and writing if they are to learn and grow at all. She was ten, desperately pained, and had been hurt severely in ways her teachers could never fully understand. She was the most miserly child I've ever known. She hoarded everything: crayons, books, feelings, even pencil stubs too short to use. She took whatever she could get, and she gave nothing in return.

Sonya wore an eloquent, stylized frown, eyebrows permanently lowered and brow deeply furrowed. Her favorite words were "Leave me alone!" and she meant it. Her pout was legendary, her temper short, and she responded to kindness by hurting herself—scratching, biting, punching her face, digging with a pencil till she bled.

Then, little by little, Sonya let me in.

Occasionally and secretly, Sonya would write her Rainbow Circle address, coloring the faint outline of a rainbow in red, orange, yellow, green, blue, and purple. Then she'd sneak glances, the shadow of a smile flitting across her pursed lips.

One day I caught her eye and smiled at her private moment of happiness. "Teach me how to make a rainbow," I said. She shredded her paper, broke each crayon into a dozen pieces, and tipped her desk over before storming to time-out.

So I launched a rainbow campaign. I left notes on rainbows, I rainbowed her work, I played rainbow songs. I overwhelmed Sonya with rainbows until there wasn't enough time in the day to destroy them all.

Her surrender—one Christmas—was absolute, and lightened the whole classroom. I became her rainbow confederate. The former Ms. Cantankerous lit up when she saw me, and her transformation made coming to work each day worthwhile.

But Sonya resented my wife with a passion. She'd stick her lower lip out or just snort if Rebekah's name were so much as mentioned. "Mr. Derek" was her special friend, and Sonya did not share. When I suggested she might spare a nice rainbow for Rebekah, Sonya looked me over with studied contempt, then hit me with her ruler.

An entire year rolled by before the next level of real progress. It was Christmas again, and the girl who gave nothing learned to share; she gave her richest treasure. I knew something was afoot when I caught Sonya grinning under her furrowed brow, working carefully. Eventually my friend showed up at my desk and shoved a picture into my hands. She repeated the motion several times before she finally let go, with a deep sigh, and stomped back to her seat.

I cried when I looked at her offering. The girl who could not share had given her treasure, and it wasn't even for me. Spelled out—in every bright color of the rainbow—it said: "REBEKAH—LOVE SONYA." It was her best painting and her first gift.

LOVE WAS BORN AT CHRISTMAS

"When Jesus spoke again to the people, he said, 'I am the light of the world. Whoever follows me will never walk in darkness, but will have the light of life'" (John 8:12, NIV).

When Jesus came, God transformed the world through his luminescent love.

Late one evening when the children were small, Andrew and I walked to his room to say good night. He raced for his bedside lamp and turned it off before literally diving over his bed to shut off the night-light. Next he rushed to the door and closed it tight, stuffing a pillow against the bottom to keep any light from seeping into the room.

Before I could ask exactly what he was up to, Andrew reached under his pillow and pulled out a small, round plastic globe he'd found in his box of Cap'n Crunch. He held the globe secretively in his hand. "Watch this, Daddy. This is great!" he said proudly, and slowly unclasped his hand. I looked closely, squinching my eyes. But there was nothing—just darkness and the vague shape of the ball.

Christ intends to shine through me, but I am often hard-pressed to see any light at all unless I squint real hard.

"Just a minute," Andrew said, and opened his door a fraction of an inch while he waved the globe slowly in the direction of the hall light. He rushed into the darkest corner of his closet and, after a lot of looking, I was able to pick out a faint glow.

"It glows in the dark! Isn't that great?" Andrew announced, then he rushed off to find a brighter light to recharge his treasure.

It occurred to me that Christmas faith often operates according to similar principles. Make a lot of noise about Advent and expectation, get as close to God as I can, wave my spirit briefly in the direction of the light, and then see how much of a glow I carry around in the world where I spend my real life. Christ intends to shine through me, but I am often hard-pressed to see any light at all unless I squint real hard, and then I am not so sure it's not mostly my imagination.

Children have *a way of shedding light* on almost any issue by virtue of their openness. They tend to accept rather than reject the natural inclination we were all born with to listen to God and to pursue the intended relationship. Andrew told me he wished he could have a "tiny little flashlight" to put inside his globe, so that the toy would glow in the dark "all by itself."

Of course, that is exactly the point of God's sending the Son into the world, Christmas and every day. Immanuel—God-with-us. God is anxious to add light to every detail of our lives, beyond the constrictions and restrictions we all too often place on our faith, beyond the limitations of a small candle lit for five minutes on Christmas Eve.

It doesn't really work to wave ourselves in the light of God and then present the world with a pitiful flicker of radiance, like a barely luminous glow-in-the-dark toy from a packet of breakfast cereal. We have the opportunity to shine so clearly that our light can be perceived without a speculative imagination, as if there really is something to this Jesus, as if the Christ-light is more than the ghost of an echo of the glory we espouse.

The key is to more deliberately engage the love born at Christmas. It's the choice between a borrowed light and a light of our own. "Love was born at Christmas" speaks of a love that penetrates, a love that challenges, a love both born and grounded in the light.

If we seek to carry a light of our own, and I believe all of us do, then we must take Christ with us, for love is the only light that can shine with any integrity through our lives. The world presents ample evidence that darkness has made significant inroads into the mood of the unfolding story. Jesus is the only light with the power to work reconciliation and healing in this broken and hurting world.

The darkness is not really a question; we know only too well that it exists. The real challenge is how well we are able to glow in the dark and whether we are prepared to take the steps necessary to carry a light of our own.

Stars and Angels Gave the Sign

The stars and angels certainly made a prominent demonstration. But the question remains: do we have the clarity of vision to see such a sign?

If anything symbolizes how the modern world receives signs, it would be my reading glasses. Clouded vision is a systemic cultural malady and—as a quintessential baby boomer—I live at the epicenter of fogged-up perception. I have entered that hard-to-define murky realm described as middle age, and I'm well aware of how hard my generation seems to be working at missing the essential message of Christmas.

It all started when I turned forty. I was prowling the aisles in a mega bookstore, trying not to spill coffee on the $38 hardcovers, when I realized I simply couldn't read anymore. "Here," Rebekah said, grinning from ear to ear, "try these."

AGE AS COMEDY

I have yet to figure out what makes my inability to see such an occasion for hilarity. But any sign of aging on my part is worth a good belly laugh in our house:

- "Look, children, Daddy's having trouble getting into those old jeans!"
- "Dad, Grandpa called; he said he wants his clothes back."
- "When did you stop jogging and start simply falling forward?"
- "Hey, Dad, how long have you been spray painting the side of your head gray?"

All extremely amusing observations. But, unfortunately, and after the initial "I'm healed, I can actually see small things again," I promptly misplaced the wondrous lenses and so initiated a cycle of purchase and loss that must be record-breaking by any standard.

At first I didn't need help seeing all the time, so I came up with the bright idea of simply leaving a pair of glasses at critical locations. Hence the desk pair, the bedside pair, the work pair, and the truck pair. All invariably found their way to my truck and met swift death-by-sitting. Occasionally, lost glasses would work their way under the gas pedal to be crushed or jump out when I opened the door so I could step on them.

Next came the "hang them around my neck" phase. This one was a hoot. Apart from being accused of looking like an elderly librarian, I variously strangled myself, could not find them, got them stuck in my desk drawer, and watched them fall from their neatly tied ends in slow motion and under my feet before ultimately being smashed.

I came closest to success when I admitted I needed to wear the devices more often. *One pair*, I reasoned, *and by necessity I will always know where they are*. Who was I trying to kid? In class I often offered special rewards or extra credit to the first child to spot my missing spectacles.

Then I developed the habit of twirling them in my fingers. Centrifugal force can send a pair of reading glasses a long way when the conditions are right, and excessive handling tends to unscrew those tiny connections at the most inopportune of times.

Recently, while on vacation, I went through three pair. At one critical moment in downtown Asheville, I was forced to rely on the waiter's recommendation for the entrée. I'm sure some people like fish heads and pig entrails, but believe me when I say my timing could have been better.

Currently I have rounded up four vintage sets. Only one pair actually helps, but the left arm is hanging precariously close to disconnection. Not to worry, it's all worth it just to entertain my family.

Spiritual Clarity

I think we sometimes need spiritual glasses, vision remedies especially designed to help us see the sign the star and the angels gave in the hills over Bethlehem. Instead, we see fuzzy images of sugarplums and reindeer and Santa and snowmen and gifts—and maybe the child in the manger. It's difficult to see any details outside the limited realm of our very exclusive personal comfort levels.

Do we see the advent of Christ in this world as a means to bring God's message of reconciling love to our brothers and sisters? Or do we see it as just another way we can pad our comfort and reward ourselves with more layers of material blessing?

We live in a great big world full of desperation, people, war, plenty, joy, pain, and even hope sometimes—if only we have the eyes to see. But sometimes we don't want to see, like the couple I know who never let anyone into their house. When visitors come, they ignore the knock, keep still, and try to be quiet enough to be thought of as "out." The few times I've made it into the living room, the husband has literally scurried back to his bedroom, afraid to be engaged. Not only are they fearful of being known, they're terrified to the core of actually comprehending anything about the world around them.

With knowledge comes responsibility; with understanding comes the imperative to act; with an open heart comes the risk of being rejected.

With clear vision we run the risk of grasping something of the pain, the pathos, the truth, and the crying need. These realities ultimately define all people who have not witnessed—or allowed themselves to respond to—the sign given by the star and the angels.

The apostle Paul put it this way: "Now we see but a poor reflection as in a mirror; then we shall see face to face. Now I know in part; then I shall know fully, even as I am fully known" (1 Corinthians 13:12, NIV).

Prayer: This Advent, God, we ask that you shine through our lives. Light our often pale and drab spirits with your love. Help us to give such commitment without reservation, and take away our fear. Thank you for the confidence that you bring. Amen.

IT'S BEGINNING TO LOOK A LOT LIKE CHRISTMAS

It was just before the Passover Feast. Jesus knew that the time had come for him to leave this world and go to the Father. Having loved his own who were in the world, he now showed them the full extent of his love.

—John 13:1, NIV

When our son, Andrew, attended college in northern Virginia, he experienced his first real winter. He traipsed around Washington, toting his digital camera and having fun with his new snow boots. Then he sent us some of those touristy snapshots the uninitiated tend to take before they get their first shoeful of slush and the whole "winter-wonderland" thing goes right out the window.

He also added captions. One cutline, pasted under an inviting view of a snowy White House lawn, caught my attention: "It's beginning to look a lot like Christmas."

"I'm wondering exactly what," my Florida-raised wife, Rebekah, exclaimed, "he thinks Christmas is supposed to look like."

- Chestnuts roasting on an open fire?
- I'm dreaming of a white Christmas?
- Oh, the weather outside is frightful?
- Frosty the Snowman?
- When the snow lay round about, deep and crisp and even?
- What fun it is to ride and sing in a one-horse open sleigh?

The day my son took those pictures, I played eighteen holes of golf in a short-sleeved shirt, thank you very much; I was grateful we could at long last turn the air-conditioning off.

I grabbed a handful of recent Christmas cards to see if I could find the answer there. The first picture sported a polar bear in a bright stripy scarf; the second offered a farmhouse under a pile of the white fluffy stuff; and the third featured a beautiful cloud of shimmering snow. Several cards featured friends posing in the classic "together for Christmas" family shot, bundled up in sweaters in front of roaring fires—probably taken sometime in late summer and under protest. Next I retrieved a few variations of the familiar manger scene with a newborn child. The last of my Christmas card "random sample" featured four bells, labeled—simply— Freedom, Hope, Tradition, and Love.

This last card resonated with me, and it sums up my prayer for this Christmas season of Advent love. Actually it's not my wish but my heartfelt prayer: I pray that Christmas this year will feature the truth of the Christ-love.

WHAT CHRISTMAS REALLY LOOKS LIKE

Freedom. I live in the land of the free and the home of the brave. I can't help myself, Christmas love looks a lot like freedom. Not "free love" in a 1960s commitment-phobic, maladaptive way, but a love we are free both to express and to receive.

Not just free, but responsible—because freedom and responsibility are necessarily connected. We have a responsibility to share this freedom-oriented love with grace (as well as the obligation to receive it). It's my heartfelt prayer that the world will one day understand the relationship of freedom to authentic love.

Christmas looks like freedom—resolute and hard-won, generous and compassionate, responsible and united. My freedom cost something; and if it doesn't continue to cost something, then it easily loses its edge. To whom much is given, much is expected. It's not hard to see that I have been privileged with freedom in order to love as Christ loved. "He now showed them the full extent of his love" (John 13:1, NIV).

Hope. Hope is expectation grounded in the evidence of experience and sustained by the promise of love. Grace brought love into this world; trust translated that love into sacrifice; hope captures the victory and presents it to each one of us as the gift of opportunity. Christmas love looks a lot like hope.

Tradition. Maybe *tradition* is truly "what Christmas looks like," because the Christmas pictures that come into our minds all tend to reference our personal history. But let's face it, too many of our traditions disappoint, either because of their secular roots or the brokenness of our own family history. The image does not always match either the desire of our heart or the intention of the original gift.

Christmas love looks a lot like hope.

So I'm praying the following with regard to tradition: I pray that we will all be inspired to step deliberately into the beginnings of a new tradition—the practice of Christlike love. Let's institute a convention that knows and practices the depth of devotion and the promise of hope that entered into human experience through the birth of an infant child two thousand years ago.

Love. It is love, of course, that binds freedom, hope, and tradition together, and that adds the Christ quality. Because freedom without God's kind of love easily becomes license; hope absent agape slips into wishing; and tradition is nothing more than the institutionalization of habit unless the practice is molded by and filtered through love.

"And the greatest of these is love" (1 Cor. 13:13).

LOVE IS CONTAGIOUS

Christ's way of love is contagious. It has a way of replicating itself. This is one of the reasons we hang a wreath on our front door for all the world to see. "Look," our wreath proclaims, "we want you to know this Christmas love too." Because, at its best, the spirit of Advent reaches out and touches all people with the truth of God's redemptive love.

Our wreath is a circle; it represents the all-encompassing nature of God's proactive love. We use magnolia branches from our tree. They are a deep green, bearing witness to new life. Rebekah cuts fresh pine, a fragrant prompt that our home is a refreshing testimony to life—a truth we are reminded to advertise not only in symbol but in practice.

I want to decorate our home in ways that inspire me to adorn my life with the visible presence of God's love. It's only through me and through you that the world can understand exactly why Jesus came. We have this privilege of sharing Jesus. We have the opportunity to participate in his grace.

We're talking about an imperative for all of us to become living Advent greetings. When people want to know what Advent looks like, they are going to remember that they have been working with us, driving the streets with us, shopping with us, playing golf with us.

Freedom? Hope? Tradition? Love? What exactly is our message?

Prayer: God of love, the source of all freedom and hope, enter into our traditions with such profound meaning that the world will know exactly what Christmas looks like through the witness of our Christlike lives. In your love, we pray. Amen.

Tuesday

No Greater Love Than This

As the Father has loved me, so I have loved you; abide in my love. If you keep my commandments, you will abide in my love, just as I have kept my Father's commandments and abide in his love. . . . This is my commandment, that you love one another as I have loved you. No one has greater love than this, to lay down one's life for one's friends.

—John 15:9-10, 12-13

Years ago, though sometimes it seems like yesterday, our daughter, Naomi, was admitted to the hospital for serious abdominal surgery. At three years old, she was wonderful. Her parents, however, were basket cases! She was patient, brave, and as cooperative as she knew how to be . . . yet so desperately pitiful that it makes me cry just thinking about it.

I remember that first morning, after she had spent more than five hours with the surgical team. They rolled Naomi into recovery with all sorts of tubes coming out of all sorts of places. Her skin was pale, her eyes were droopy, and she didn't have the strength to lift her beautiful head. All she could manage was to squeeze the rear leg of her musical reindeer and produce a weak smile in response to the zany Christmas tunes the reindeer produced.

I—and here's where I get a vague sense of what Christmas love is all about—wanted so very much to take her place. I wanted to lie there for my daughter—sobbing and pained—as the nurses dressed her hurts. I wanted to have her surgery, I wanted to be stuck with her needles, and I wanted to take her place every time the doctor ordered another one of those tests. But I couldn't. All Rebekah and I could do was sit by Naomi's bedside and hold her tiny hand.

Later that week I watched Naomi sleep fitfully, her body warm in contrast to the cold steel of the hospital bed frame. Reeling from both pity and wonder, I watched the gentle rhythm of her breathing, broken only by the occasional shudder as she remembered her pain. She made the lab technician cry when he woke her and she saw his needle.

"Don't you hurt me, please," she said, fixing the unfortunate man with those enormous brown eyes; she squeezed a big tear from both corners at once. I had to reassure him first, then Naomi.

PERFECT LOVE

"No one has greater love than this, to lay down one's life for one's friends. You are my friends if you do what I command you" (John 15:13-14). Christ chose to be born into this dark world as a helpless baby in the care of a nondescript refugee family. He chose the course that ultimately would lead to a brutal and torturous death on a cruel cross. Jesus is able to do for us what we are not able to do for ourselves—what I was not able to do for Naomi.

Jesus is able to do for us what we are not able to do for ourselves.

Thinking about that night in the hospital, I remember that Jesus came for other children too. Three rooms down the hall, two-year-old "Sharon" whimpered in the dark, without a parent's comforting touch. Sharon's life had not been easy, and she received nourishment through a tube attached to her stomach. She was reluctant to grasp the finger I offered; the nurse could only say the toddler had good reason to be afraid of men. Sharon slept alone, and I wondered where she would go when she left the hospital.

Still curled up, stunningly beautiful even in sleep, our daughter, Naomi, draped her arm carefully around her bright red corduroy pig (also scheduled for surgery). She caressed the stuffed head, oh so gently, while the musical reindeer observed from his cozy spot under the crook of her arm. Sharon slept too, her golden curls flung carelessly across her pillow, a borrowed teddy bear keeping silent watch. Most of the third floor lay quiet and slumbering, and I felt an odd sense of peace there, for all the hurting and the pain.

PRAYER AND LOVE

Prayer filled our daughter's room. Silent and spoken, thought or as yet unthought, written and telephoned, corporate and alone; prayers full with faith and prayers strong from hearts full with love; prayers squeezed out from minds that scarcely believed; and prayers that flowed from the substance of certain conviction.

I still fail to even barely understand how all this works, but I do remember being broken under the truth of the love. And, extraordinary as it may seem, I know without a doubt that lives—Naomi's, Sharon's, mine—were changed somehow because of it, and that the children slept in a measure of peace.

It's easy to have our emotions stretched at times like these. Rebekah and I were forced to watch helplessly while our three-year-old child experienced pain that she could not understand. But such knowing cannot change the reality and substance of the comforting knowledge of Christmas love. What power is set in motion when people share a common conviction, I honestly do not know. But I do know God initiated that chain of prayerful power two thousand years ago in the context of Advent love, and my Savior communicated peace to me that night. And I am full with the truth of it.

Prayer: Lord Jesus, God-with-us, you were willing to suffer terribly so that we might avoid the pain of separation from the source of love. Help us to comprehend the depth of your Advent love and the scope of your amazing grace. Amen.

WEDNESDAY

AFFIRMED WITH A LOVE
BEYOND TIME AND SPACE

In this is love, not that we loved God but that he loved us and sent his
Son to be the atoning sacrifice for our sins. Beloved, since God loved us
so much, we also ought to love one another.

—1 John 4:10-11

When I look at your heavens, the work of your fingers,
    the moon and the stars that you have established;
what are human beings that you are mindful of them,
    mortals that you care for them?
Yet you have made them a little lower than God,
    and crowned them with glory and honor.

—Psalm 8:3-5

Somewhere, in the section of my brain that stores images, I can see
one of those insightful cartoons that holds unintended theological
truth. I don't remember the artist or the era, but I do recall a man gazing incredulously into the night sky, the firmament bright and ablaze
with light and glory.

"This all makes me feel so insignificant," the man sighs. "What do you
think?"

"I agree," replies his companion, with neither empathy nor tact. "I
think you're insignificant too."

The assessment, of course, is 100 percent wrong. Such thinking fails
to take into account a loving God who is in love with creation. In the con-

text of God's immense, boundless, incalculable love, the unfathomable universe tells us a much different story. Sometimes, like the cartoon character, I too look wonderingly into the deep night sky, but I experience an overwhelming sense of how remarkably *significant* it all makes me feel.

"What are human beings that you are mindful of them?" the psalmist asks. Well, it follows that we must be something special. In the face of all that beauty and awe and the hugeness of it all, the real wonder is not that God loves me, but that God loves enough to think about Derek Maul, that God is concerned about each individual reading this page, and that God sent Jesus for our personal redemption.

We are affirmed so completely because we are chosen so specifically. The Creator of this vast, glorious universe chooses to reveal love for people as individual human beings. We are God's personal children. We surely are significant, and we certainly are loved.

LOVE SO IMMENSE

God's love is huge, and our Creator has a reach so enormous that sometimes I have trouble wrapping my mind around even the small parts of the wonder I can see.

Our world is a marvel that I can't begin to imagine. We're hurtling through space at speeds close to 70,000 miles per hour (it's a wonder we don't all fall off!); the entire planet spins at over 1,000 miles per hour at the equator; our rotation, believe it or not, is slowing down; and the orbit our home transcribes around the sun routinely wobbles in relation to the gravitational forces of other planets.

What we understand as "time" simply describes a relationship among these and many other variables. Time in actual fact is neither absolute nor completely verifiable. Our understanding is hampered by the reality that minutes and days and hours and months are relative terms, fractions of whatever a year happens to be during the journey of one set of spinning, careening orbs in relation to another. Curiously, most people believe that the earth returns—like clockwork—to a particular fixed point in space exactly every 365.25 days.

Consider the following:

- More than two thousand years ago, the Julian calendar began with a 445-day "correction" year.
- In 1752 the British Parliament eliminated a big chunk of September in order to align with the Gregorian calendar of 1582.
- Today we quantify time via some fifty atomic clocks programmed to record the atomic oscillations of a metal called cesium. The calendar year is now officially measured as 290,091,200,500,000,000 oscillations of Cs.

WHO, EXACTLY, IS IN CONTROL?

We seem to be trying to craft a world where people depend on the illusion of control. But there's a fly in our ointment: we are not alone in this universe. We are unutterably significant certainly, but it's not because of us; it's because of great love. The amazing God of creation loves us.

Those stargazing cartoon characters missed the truth about significance in part because of limited perspective. It's an easy trap to fall into, especially considering that even the language we speak limits us conceptually. The metaphors, the illustrations, and the examples we use are necessarily lifted from life here on earth; our outlook is bound by both time and space. Even the best science-fiction authors must write within the confines of our earthbound vocabulary. And we can describe God only in the narrow vernacular of our small planet.

PERSPECTIVE

Humans have always looked to the stars, and for the past two decades we've been privileged to enjoy the view from the Hubble Space Telescope (placed in service 1990). The orbiting observatory looks out, far away from our home, deep into the as-yet unknown. The farther into space the telescope peers, the more questions it reveals; the more we know about the scope of creation, the less of its totality we understand.

Adam and Eve (Genesis 1–4) were seduced by a misplaced desire "to be like God"; they immediately put themselves front and center as if creation were all about them. It's not so much that they weren't significant as that they so easily forgot the source of their meaning. When Adam and Eve abandoned the reality of a day-by-day relationship to the Eternal, they forgot who they were.

So here we are, getting ready for Christmas, engaging what it means to live in this twenty-first century, and too often we attempt to accomplish the task outside our relationship to God. We fail to address, through faith, what we know only "in part" (1 Cor. 13:12), "through a glass, darkly" (KJV).

Christmas helps me to peer with unparalleled wonder into eternity; and Advent reveals a most profound and unsearchable truth that is confirmed every time we grasp the infinite and gaze into the heavens: "In this is love, not that we loved God but that [God] loved us" (1 John 4:10).

Prayer: Eternal and unfathomable God, we acknowledge the limits of our own imagination and intelligence. Please accompany us in our struggle to understand how much you love us, and as we attempt to apply that understanding to our lives. We ask in the name of Jesus, the one who meets us as individuals, the one who reveals the extent of your great and abiding love. Amen.

THURSDAY

A NEW AND LIVING WAY

He said to him the third time, "Simon son of John, do you love me?"
Peter felt hurt because he said to him the third time, "Do you love me?"
And he said to him, "Lord, you know everything; you know that I love
you." Jesus said to him, "Feed my sheep."

—John 21:17

Some people have trouble bringing themselves to say, "I love you."
They're fearful of the phrase and shy away, as if the words will
cause some kind of damage on their way out. It's as if they dare not
risk what love might require of them in the way of emotion had they
but the courage to speak it out loud. So they take great pains to shut
themselves off.

It's a loss that makes me sad—sad for them and sad for those of us
who need to understand we are worth that kind of risk—especially when
we consider the New Testament principle: "Perfect love casts out fear" (1
John 4:18).

The purity of this Advent journey relates directly to our willingness to
connect with God's kind of love without compromise. Over two thousand years ago—as measured in the time ascribed to this world—God did
something brand-new in the way of faithful love. Christmas marks God's
breaking into time and space. That's the Incarnation, God putting on flesh
and blood, when love entered this world in a "new and living way" (Heb.
10:20). Immanuel; God-with-us; God loving us. And—way too important for any of us to gloss over—God teaching us how to love.

THE CHALLENGE

Love is a most remarkable phenomenon. We are continually challenged to understand more completely what God was up to in the way of love, and then to get on board in ways that fundamentally change us, change our orientation to life as we experience the real world from day to day.

When we talk about love, my mind is drawn to the conversation Jesus had with his friend Peter that tense morning when they met on the Galilean shore, just a short while after the Resurrection (John 21). Jesus the teacher, very much conscious that his followers were still struggling to grasp just what his time with them was all about, threw this piercing question at his apprentice with deliberate insistency. "Do you love me, Peter?" "Do you love me, Peter?" "Do you love me, Peter?"

Sometimes Jesus fixes me with that same penetrating gaze. I squirm as he poses the incisive query; I can hardly withstand the purity of his love.

In this twenty-first-century culture, we tend to play fast and loose with our application of the word *love*. So much so that sometimes I find myself wanting to discard the expression and come up with another word entirely new—something unmistakably rooted in the truth behind the question Jesus fired at Peter. I've made this point before, but it's worth repeating. The moniker *Christian* has likewise been misused and distorted, and now I often refer to myself as a *Christ-follower*, a *Jesus-follower*, or a *traveler of the Way*.

THE FOUNDATION OF LOVE

Relationships usually lie at the heart of our understanding of love, and we all learn our personal truth in the context of everyday experience. Consequently, much of what I know about God's love—and the lessons remain both challenging and ongoing—is deeply rooted in relationships of long-term faithfulness that have been defined by resolute promise and authentic commitment.

My life has been full with faithful committed love, and it has been from the moment I was born. Even the possibility of my birth was front-loaded with expectant promise and fervent prayer. I was loved well before the day I was born in the upstairs bedroom on Dolphins Road, and I have been fortunate enough to see those models remain intact over the years. *Love, in my experience, has always been long-term and ironclad.*

ROOTED IN PROMISE

The rootedness and security of my experiences growing up enabled me to engage my later chosen relationships out of the understanding that unions of love are forever. Consequently, God; my wife, Rebekah; and our children could enter my life on those terms.

Because I grew up knowing beyond a shadow of a doubt that my parents would be there for me, unfailingly, love for me finds its most definitive genesis in faithfulness and consistency. Love was always something rock solid that transcended mood or moment. Because of that linchpin, all the more subtle, exotic, or emotional features find meaning in the context of commitment, the consistency of promise, and the framework of time.

Growing up, I attended church and Sunday school, and I found out about God's constancy long before I accepted Jesus as Savior and Lord. I knew God loved me without any conditions attached, even if I did not want anything to do with God. I knew Christ was willing to die for me if that was what it would take to break down the barriers between us. I learned to love God the same way the Creator loves me—unconditionally.

So when my first girlfriend ditched me—at age sixteen—I was genuinely puzzled.

"Why?" I asked.

"Because we can't just go on forever," she replied logically.

To which I responded, logically for me, "Why not?"

Even though I had it all wrong in terms of how dating works, I had one essential idea exactly right. To me, commitment was the cornerstone of relationships.

Today, Rebekah and I continue to celebrate commitment with all sorts of important anniversaries in addition to our wedding day. These include our first date, the first "I love you," and the day we became engaged, to name but a few.

LOVE IS A CELEBRATION!

This may sound corny, but Rebekah and I really do pounce on just about any reason to celebrate the fact that we are together and that we are in love. We believe love is well defined as celebration, and that, in the decision to celebrate, we're going to find more reason to love.

Christmas celebration works on the same principle. We celebrate God's radical commitment to love us, and we celebrate extravagantly. We find that in doing so, our joyful response to God's love strengthens our commitment to new life in Christ. It's a positive cycle, and the truth of it says a lot about the power of commitment in sustaining love. I can say without hesitation that love is much more than romantic feelings—which fluctuate; love is more than common interests—which are certainly fun but are not enough to be foundational; love is more than good intentions, more than phone calls, letters, sugar-free chocolates, flowers, balloons, or even a perfect cup of coffee delivered in bed every morning.

Love may be all these things, certainly, but if love were just one thing, it would have to be commitment.

If love were just one thing, it would have to be commitment.

MOST OF ALL, LOVE IS COMMITMENT

Commitment is about keeping promises, and it is about keeping faith. Committed love is enumerated in the thousands of seemingly small choices we make from day to day in the particulars of our lives. That's true in the way we relate to one another, and it's life-changingly true in terms of our moment-by-moment decision to follow Christ.

For Rebekah, and for me, commitment means still dating (each other!) at least one day in every week, and it means deliberately attending to numerous details every time the sun comes up. We understand now that love makes constant choices. We make literally scores of decisions each and every day, choices that help to flesh out and to fill in the details of what it means to love. We chose each other long ago, but we continue that process in the present tense because *love* is—at its best—an action word. Love entails the choice to share absolutely everything, and it calls us continually to pledge ourselves to each other's evolving identity as beloved children of God.

COMMITTED LOVE IS AN ACT OF FAITH

Love also means making the choice to grow together in our faith. God's action in the world is not confined to history; God seeks to express agape love in and through our relationships and our homes. Love means offering our spouse, our children, and one day our grandchildren the gift of genuine commitment in the framework of family rather than a fabricated or propped-up façade. Love means faithful friendships; love means constancy in our role as children, aunts, uncles, and siblings; love means commitment to our community, because that is the venue where God expects us to feed those sheep God loves so very much.

Commitment takes time and energy and resources and honesty and patience and so much more moment-by-moment attention because we all are worth every ounce of it. For my family, commitment is the foundation of relationships; it always has been. And the way we feel about God is pivotal because God sets the standard for unconditional love, through a personal commitment to us. God sent Jesus, the promise of the ages, to set love into motion. "And the Word became flesh and lived among us, and we have seen his glory, the glory as of a father's only son, full of grace and truth" (John 1:14).

Love also means making the choice to grow together in our faith.

Only through God can we make such promise work in our own relationships. So that *whoever trusts will have* the opportunity to know God's level of committed love forever. God's love is a river of life flowing constantly, and God desires us to experience the healing focus of redeeming love in absolutely every situation. Now that's Christmas for you.

Prayer: Teacher and Guide, the impact of your love on our lives is amazing. Help us respond more completely to this miracle and share your message of faithful love with your world. Help us in our commitment to involve you more thoroughly in our personal and family lives. Guide our thoughts, our actions, and our decisions to the course of your will. Bless us with your peace that is beyond our understanding. In the name of Jesus. Amen.

FRIDAY

GOD IS THE STRONGEST!
ORDINARY FAMILY; EXTRAORDINARY GOD

> There is therefore now no condemnation for those who are in Christ
> Jesus. For the law of the Spirit of life in Christ Jesus has set you free from
> the law of sin and of death. For God has done what the law, weakened
> by the flesh, could not do: by sending his own Son.
> —Romans 8:1-3

In contemporary culture, love is often portrayed as a weakness—a malady or sickness that saps potency, resolve, will, and strength. The correct clinical term for that assessment, a psychologist once told me, is *hooey*. My experience reflects an entirely opposite picture of love. Love is strong, so strong that it can withstand any kind of evil that might come along.

My friend Craig is a general in the United States Army—Special Forces, Army Rangers, that kind of thing. On the day he and his family joined the church, his four children were baptized, and the event quickly turned into one of those "multiple-tissue" Sunday mornings. Craig has been in life-and-death situations most of us could never imagine; he's the guy you'd want to take along if you needed extra confidence, the kind of quiet hero who keeps this nation free. He's strong, he's a terrific leader, and he's tough; but if you had been in church that day, you would have seen a kind of strength that belies what most people think about might and valor—and what we too often believe about love.

People understand—if only from reading my newspaper column—

that my family comprises a very real American household. By "real" I mean that, just like the rest of the world, we have our ups and our downs, our miscommunications and our fights, our times of harmony and our times of dissonance, our energy and our fatigue, our pain and our tears. Then, of course, we also have our days when everything falls so beautifully into place it feels like a dream.

I wrote in my journal about one such Advent Saturday, when the children were teens. I first noticed something unusual when I caught the warring siblings talking pleasantly about how best to arrange some Christmas decorations. Andrew actually invited his sister into his room to share the details of a project he was working on for a gift, and then Naomi pleasantly asked if he wanted to share her ice cream.

Later, Andrew did a couple of loads of laundry without being asked, and after that Naomi cleaned the kitchen. Now do you understand why I made special note of the day? The aura of family harmony was palpable, and I couldn't help but smile, wondering exactly what events had precipitated such an occurrence. And was there a way to guarantee— beyond scheduling Christmas more often—that such cooperative love might possibly happen again?

OUT OF THE MOUTHS OF BABES

When our children were young, they tended to annotate good days with disarmingly insightful comments. Later, their self-conscious teenage perspective put the brakes on such beguiling charm. These earlier declarations were nuggets of truth, glimpses of wonder we knew we would treasure for a long time, as indeed we have.

I remember one wet December evening at the end of such a day. We finished eating and shared our family devotions, reading an Advent passage from the Gospel of Luke. Christmas was in the air, presents were beginning to accumulate, and we were all talking happily. Rebekah and I were thoroughly enjoying the moment. We held hands, leaning in on each other; she rested her head on my shoulder; we kissed.

A quiet voice broke in from across the table. "Mama, Daddy, I love it when you do that. Don't move. I'll be right back."

We didn't move. Andrew returned with Rebekah's camera around his neck, her Pentax ME Super SLR complicated grown-up camera. He wound on, focused, and took a very steady existing-light exposure. He said that he wanted a picture of us "just like that" to put on the shelf in his room and, please, to get it developed "pronto."

We went on with our evening; I think the children were six and eight at the time. Homework, then stories, bed, lights-out, and quiet. All in perfect, stress-free rhythm. Scary easy, not what we were used to. Naomi, as per her usual, was fast asleep in seconds.

Then, as I was leaving Andrew's room, almost safely down the hall and back in the kitchen with Rebekah, I heard the familiar "Daddy, come back. I've got something else to tell you." And I thought that, well, the evening must have been too much of a good thing. He's trying to stall; it's the same old same stretch-it-out tactic, and I'll end up getting mad. But this time I decided to give him credit because of the good day, so I stuck my head back into the darkened room.

"What's up, Andrew?"

"You know what, Daddy?"

"What, Andrew?"

"I love you. You are a good daddy."

And that was all. I never heard another peep!

Like I said, we are an ordinary family. There's not much that is so wonderful or so terrible that it overwhelms us. Mostly life turns out to be—you know—the nitty-gritty of ups and downs and normal everyday events we share and deal with and then move on. But there is nothing average about the love that binds us all together. There is nothing average about the commitment Rebekah and I have for each other. There is nothing average about our God or about Jesus or the extraordinarily amazing cascade of possibilities that he introduced to this world that first Christmas.

> *There is nothing average about our God or about Jesus or the extraordinarily amazing cascade of possibilities that he introduced to this world that first Christmas.*

CONTEXT

It has to be this Christmas-powered love that makes all the difference. Christmas-powered love is the epicenter of my strength. Its power infuses me when I need to understand what God is up to, what God wants to be up to in and through my life. The powerful redemptive truth of Christmas love enables me to realize what an astonishing gift this life together as a resurrection community can be.

So long, that is, as I pay attention, and so long as I allow God to speak to me through the wonder of our most ordinary of lives together.

EPILOGUE

One more thing happened on that redemptive evening etched in my journal, a powerful memory that still lingers in my mind and heart today. The children were asleep; Rebekah and I had enjoyed our tea together; and the evening slipped into night. Much later, after I had walked the dog and put out the garbage and locked up the house, I attended to my usual list of late-night details before brushing my teeth and crawling into bed. The lights were off, the blinds were closed, and the kitchen was clean—everything pretty much in the proper place.

The house seemed extra quiet as I tiptoed down the creaky wooden hallway from Naomi's room after taking a long look at both sleeping children; it's a joy that can still cap off my day so beautifully when we are fortunate enough to have them home. As I crept away, almost out of earshot, I heard Naomi—half-asleep and into the stillness: "Daddy, I love you. Daddy, I do love God; God is the strongest. Good night."

And she fell back into sleep again. God is the strongest.

You bet God is strong. Yes, God loves me that way; God loves all of us that way. Even our children knew it, when they were so young and we lived on Piedmont Road, way back at the beginning of time. It's one of the reasons I can say with utmost confidence that while our average family does indeed have average experiences every average day, we know with a nonaverage certainty that God loves us, that our God is the strongest—so much stronger than the strong—and that God's strength is a powerful and a sturdy love.

We know that this love is a strong love and that we are exceptional because of that fact. We are God's children, and absolutely nothing in the universe can possibly compromise that kind of powerful, life-changing, loving, strongest-of-Christmas truths.

Prayer: We approach you as humble people, God. We feel blessed; we feel supported; and we are encouraged by our knowledge of your strong love for us. It's comforting to realize that your commitment to us is far stronger than the limits of our faith. We pray because we love you, and because we want to know you more completely. Amen.

TWICE WRAPPED IN BANDS OF CLOTH

This will be a sign for you: you will find a child wrapped in bands of cloth and lying in a manger.

—Luke 2:12

So Joseph took the body and wrapped it in a clean linen cloth and laid it in his own new tomb, which he had hewn in the rock.

—Matthew 27:59-60

I have read some exceptional books in recent years regarding the language of love. Language, of course, is simply a vehicle for communication. Sometimes, especially when it comes to a reality as powerful as love, the words at our disposal are not nearly up to the job of getting across such an important message.

Words are great, and words are certainly worth the effort, but words are only a part of the equation. Even the best collection of words can be like standing on the other side of a room holding a sign that reads "Hug!" rather than actually delivering the warm embrace via genuine physical contact.

Immanuel means "God-with-us"; it's God's love language in the most profound way, and it takes the expression to new levels previously unimagined. Jesus often told his followers that he had no intention of doing away with anything the law required. Instead, Christ pointed out that his purpose in coming was and is to fulfill God's guidelines completely (Matt. 5:17). Immanuel, God-with-us, is the definitive presence of God's love in a way that transcends the limitations inherent in mere words.

Not some sign held up at a distance.

Not even the best of words.

Jesus is God's HUG.

FOR EXAMPLE

Recently two members of my small-group Bible study at church lost their eldest son in a tragic accident. Just a few days later my friend Gary was invited to spend the evening at their home.

"I don't think I can go," Gary said. "I have no idea what to say."

"Don't worry," I told him. "There are no words that could be anywhere near as powerful as your physical presence. Just being there will speak volumes."

I honestly believe God's love language is revealed more often in presence than in solution. At church recently a member of my adult Sunday school class wanted to talk. When we sat down together, all her grief and pain started to pour out. We talked for a long time and then, for some foolish reason, I wanted to have something clever or insightful to say.

"Let's pray together," I said. "I'm going to ask God to take away your pain, to heal your hurts, and to make everything right again. . . ."

How shallow! I'm embarrassed at myself once again just writing it down.

Fortunately, my friend possessed a grace equal to the challenge, although for a moment I entertained the possibility that she might smack me as hard as she could. She grabbed both my hands and looked into my eyes. "I don't need for God to make everything fine again," she said, teeth gritted and tear-filled eyes boring deep into my soul. "I just need to know that God is here with me, and that God is holding my hand."

She understood the meaning of Immanuel more clearly than I did.

THE MOMENT OF BIRTH

If Christmas love is cradled in the birth of Christ, then I know from personal experience that the original "Holy Night" had to have been one tough midnight shift for Mary and Joseph. The passages of our two children into this world were events of great beauty, but they were also occasions defined by pain. Like anything worthwhile, Christmas love came into this world kicking and screaming, strained to the limit, and probably gasping for breath.

Our son, Andrew, was born—serendipitously—on Father's Day. We actually expected our bundle of joy on Memorial Day weekend in May, so the month of June 1982 goes into the books as long and excruciating. Four weeks late—and counting—took some of the poetry out of the Father's Day timing. By the time we drove to the hospital, our reality involved more a desperate sense of, "Please, oh please, let's get this over and done with" than a serene, "Oh, joy, it's Father's Day; this certainly is a Hallmark moment."

Nonetheless, that first birth stands in my mind as maybe the most poignant and heartrending moment in my life. Bright orange hair, purple body—indignant at the trauma of it all—impatient already to begin this new adventure of life. Then, almost instantly, relaxed and content; transferred from my incredulous arms to his mother's; love personified without the necessity of a single word.

THE BIRTH OF PROMISE

Later, when Andrew graduated from high school, I published the following "Open Letter to My Son" as a letter to the editor in the *Tampa Tribune*:

Dear Son:

A lot of people tell their graduates: "It seems like only yesterday I held you as a baby." Let's not go there; we both know it was an eternity. Because before that eternity we didn't have children, and I was not a father. Not being a father is something beyond my ability to conceptualize at this point of my life.

There is so much that these past eighteen years have made possible. It's almost as if my life had been on cruise control, safely below the speed limit, and then you came along and it was suddenly wide open, full throttle, maximum volume, disruptive enough that I am quite happy to mix metaphors and still not even begin to approach the meaning of it all.

You have, I believe, stretched us to the limit, even beyond at times. Yet I would not exchange the experience of raising such a son for anything in the world. I remember second grade, when your sainted teacher tried to explain why she enjoyed you so much. "Some teachers would treasure a class full of Sandees," she said. (Sandee was perfect: well-behaved, nice handwriting, and flawless A's on every piece of work.) "But that would bore me to tears. Your Andrew keeps me on my toes, and I do so enjoy a real challenge."

I couldn't have said it better myself. But what a challenge; the opportunity to know and love and nurture a child who came into this world screaming, "I am an individual!" at the top of his lungs.

Yet who else would have taken on a leading citizen and his stable of attorneys at age eleven to permanently rid Pensacola's waterfront of floating billboards? What other child might have caused family adjustments so far-reaching that it helped all of us grow in ways we could never have imagined? And what else could have forced me to my knees so often that my relationship with the living God became central to my life?

You see, these two amazing decades have been the catalyst for a family that hasn't been afraid to thrive through eighteen years of children, rather than cave in and go belly-up. When God placed you in our young household, he intended such creativity and growth because he knew that this was not a home that would ever settle for anything less.

And that is where we leave it to you, Andrew. We leave the potentiality and possibility of a life charged and packed with the resourceful spirit of the Creator in your eighteen-year-old grasp. God has given us so much, and all he asks of you is to allow him to continue to be your guide. May you know peace, promise, and the grace of perfect joy, in the name of him who is able to keep you from stumbling, the only wise God.

I do so love you,

Daddy

In the Name of Christmas Love

Birth and death. Christ engaged both difficult passages in the name of Christmas love. Each Christmas and Easter, our church prepares a special service of music designed to present God's message in a fresh way. It's my privilege to play the part of narrator, and the experience has always been, for me, powerful.

In 2007, during Palm Sunday worship, I stood at the pulpit to read from Matthew's account of the Crucifixion, including chapter 27, verses 57-60: "When it was evening, there came a rich man from Arimathea, named Joseph, who was also a disciple of Jesus. He went to Pilate and asked for the body of Jesus; then Pilate ordered it to be given to him. So Joseph took the body and wrapped it in a clean linen cloth and laid it in his own new tomb, which he had hewn in the rock. He then rolled a great stone to the door of the tomb and went away."

All I could think about in that moment was Christ's birth that night in the stable at Bethlehem. I thought about the fact that Jesus was even then wrapped in bands of cloth. I thought about the echo of his entry into this world, resonant in his exit into eternity. I had not considered this thought before and—I could not help myself—I wept.

> "This will be a sign for you: you will find a child wrapped in bands of cloth and lying in a manger" (Luke 2:12).

God must have shed bitter tears as he watched Jesus—once again—being wrapped in bands of cloth and placed so lovingly in the resting place that had been prepared.

This is love. This is Christmas. This is why Jesus came.

Prayer: I can hardly fathom the extent of a love that would choose to be born into the promise of such a brutal future. You are that sacrifice, Lord; please accept our grateful love. Amen.

Week 4

JOY

Overture to Joy

Go Tell It on the Mountain

The shepherds returned, glorifying and praising God for all they had heard and seen, as it had been told them.

—Luke 2:20

Until Christmas 2005, I'd managed to live my entire life without ever seeing a burlesque reindeer. My lucky streak came to an end when my friend Tim managed to bring one home from a church ornament gift exchange. Plastic, gaudy, and about four inches tall, the creature sported what can only be described as a pink boa and a tutu.

My friend's wife, ever quick of wit, immediately announced they had a "stripper reindeer."

"That's why on our Christmas tree we have what we call 'the wall side,'" I observed. "Over the years it's interesting to see what ends up back there."

"Not at all," Kelly replied. "I think it'll make a great conversation piece."

I did my best to warn them. This was only Tim and Kelly's second Christmas together; they were going be surprised at how easy it is to set unintentional precedent. Today's novelty could become next year's trend. Lifelong collections have been initiated with less. What's next, the alluring yet repulsive glowing table lamp clad in fishnet stockings from the classic movie *A Christmas Story*? By the time they enter middle age, my friends could well be identified in Christmas lore as "the people who collect bawdy ornaments."

In my house we call such aggregations our "un-collections": sets of related items we never intended to amass, yet, somehow, there they are. You know how it goes. One year someone gave my wife a small angel. She left it on her desk just long enough to attract a companion. "How nice, she has an angel collection," someone said the next day. Before long we had to buy them their own tree.

In her office at church Rebekah has around twenty-five teapots. I grew up in England where it's a time-honored practice to interrupt important sporting events to serve tea. Additionally, drinking tea together is a meaningful ritual in our marriage. Now throw in the fact that my wife really does like creative ceramics. Need I say more? There's a difference, however, between collecting artistic pottery and having to smile a gracious thank-you when someone hands off a polka-dotted orange ceramic box with a spout, and calls it a "collector's edition English teapot."

This year I'm seriously considering leaving two or three twenty-dollar bills in a decorative grouping next to my computer. I can't wait to see what happens to my new collection once a few thousand readers catch on.

ICONIC CELEBRATION

A red octagon means "Stop!" Golden arches make us think about hamburgers. A set of scales suggests the balance of justice. Our culture is chock-full of icons, graphic symbols, and picture images that bring specific ideas to mind. With today's emphasis on a constant stream of media images, America is loaded with these interesting logos, and at this time of year, Christmas is iconic in a big way.

Fat Santas, bells, elves, stars, trees, angels, dollar signs, brightly wrapped presents, candy canes, festively packaged booze, shepherds, tutu-clad plastic reindeer, snowflakes, manger scenes. What images, I wonder, best symbolize the holidays in our celebrations as individuals and families?

I was churning the idea around in my head the evening my wife and I stopped by the church for the annual preschool Christmas program. If you haven't attended such an event, I recommend it; nothing could be better for the soul. The kids may have been cute, but their parents were a hoot. The church was packed with twenty-five- to forty-year-olds. Then, when the children paraded down the aisle, the camcorders came out en masse. It seemed more than half the audience was watching the live event from somewhere else, peering intently into hundreds of tiny two-inch screens.

I often object to the notion that "Christmas is for the children," because Christmas is so profoundly for the rest of us too.

Imagine a crowd of preschoolers, dressed up in their Christmas best, singing their little hearts out at the top of their lungs. Imagine the Christmas story, often incomprehensible to those who will not hear, told simply by clear young voices, chanting their favorite lines in chorus, joy dancing in the brightness of their eyes. Imagine unbounded preschool joy.

Talk about a most appropriate seasonal icon.

I often object to the notion that "Christmas is for the children," because Christmas is so profoundly for the rest of us too. But I have to confess that children often do a better job than sophisticates when it comes to telling the story and when it comes to cutting through the detritus to reveal the essential unavoidable truth.

GLORIFYING AND PRAISING GOD

As the program wound down, the preschool director asked those of us in the audience to help out with the last song. "You sing the verses," she said. "The children will handle the chorus."

The song started tamely enough. Grown-ups can be self-conscious, and it's tough to read music while squinting into a camcorder. The children, however, had no such hang-ups. They were more than happy to simply experience the moment. Their part came, and the pianist played the distinctive chord that set up the refrain.

"GO, TELL IT ON THE MOUNTAIN," fifty kids fairly roared, drowning out the technology-focused adults with their enthusiasm and their unqualified belief.

Go, tell it on the mountain? We didn't need to. The children already had.

JOY AS OUR CHRISTMAS LOGO

When my daughter—the then future Naomi Campbell—reached a certain point in her relationship with my favorite son-in-law—Craig Campbell—it wasn't difficult for the rest of us to see where things were ultimately headed. Children don't always tell their parents everything, but mothers and dads typically have the ability to know the truth regardless.

Sometimes such insight is wisdom difficult to bear. Sometimes the dark experiences pierce a parent's soul with a clarity that is quite literally excruciating. But we are perceptive when it comes to joy too. And that, probably more than any other reason, is why we love Craig. Naomi wore joy in his presence or even just talking about him—and she still does—as an icon representative of their new relationship.

Likewise, the coming of Jesus is the advent of joy. Joy is my Christmas icon.

IS THAT ALL THERE IS?

I once interviewed a woman who tried to explain why she decided to start a family. "My husband and I were sitting around on Christmas morning, opening presents," she said. "It didn't last that long. I looked around and said, 'Is this all there is?'"

"Well, there's only so much mileage in wrapping paper," I said. "Joy is something different entirely." Then we talked a little about what makes Christmas work for my family.

The interviewee didn't have any clue regarding Christ-based Christmas joy. She wanted to extend the gift-giving part, and she knew she wanted something more. She also understood that children are more closely connected to that elusive "something," even while she resolutely failed to realize that honest-to-goodness Christmas joy can be hers just as profoundly.

The preschool children singing their hearts out had no such existential dilemma. They're always ready to "go tell it on the mountain" at the drop of a hat, gifts or no gifts. People who know Jesus wear joy as a badge, much the same way our daughter, Naomi, winsomely advertises her love for Craig.

The shepherds returned glorifying and praising God because they had met Jesus Christ that day. There is no Christmas to celebrate without that kind of encounter, and certainly no joy for anyone to go tell on the mountain.

Prayer: Thanks so much, Lord God, for such a message that we can share. Thank you for joy, and thank you for the compelling reality of your kind of joy at this amazing time of year. "Go, tell it on the mountain, over the hills and everywhere; go, tell it on the mountain, that Jesus Christ is born."* Amen.

* John W. Work Jr. (1872–1925)

Fourth Sunday of Advent

Certainty

For God did not give us a spirit of cowardice, but rather a spirit of power
and of love and of self-discipline. . . . But I am not ashamed, for I know
the one in whom I have put my trust, and I am sure that he is able to
guard until that day what I have entrusted to him. . . . Guard the good
treasure entrusted to you, with the help of the Holy Spirit living in us.
—2 Timothy 1:7, 12, 14

One December night after a frenzied evening of Christmas shopping, I walked out of the local supermarket balancing three
overstuffed bags of groceries. Stumbling over my tangled shoelaces, I
fell into the back panel of my long-suffering car, adding another small
dent to the collage. I brushed aside the growing pile of stuff on the
backseat to make room for the groceries, caught sight of myself in the
rearview mirror, and realized I needed to shave. My hair was dirty, and
my shirt was fastened incorrectly, one button off all the way down.

Closing the passenger door, seat belt still hanging out, I noticed an
attractive-looking couple ease across the parking lot, buttons and snaps all
in place. She could have passed for Julia Roberts, and he looked like Brad
Pitt or a slick TV news anchor. Flashing Hollywood smiles at the bag-boy,
they glided smoothly to their spotless BMW coupe, apple red with the
top rolled back. Spick-and-span as the owners themselves, it cruised
effortlessly into the night on shiny black tires that seemed to repel dirt like
matched poles on two magnets. I could hear the musical sound of their
laughter through the night air as I climbed into my dirty car. I closed the
door on my finger.

I passed them again at the light on Bloomingdale Avenue, perfect sets of teeth glinting in the light, fashionable clothes setting off the effect, big hair unaffected by the breeze, holding hands.

Nobody has the right to be that shiny, that good-looking, that smooth, that naturally poised. I know I'm not. Maybe they were cable network televangelists; maybe they were filming some kind of commercial. . . . Maybe I was just a little bit jealous?

MAKING ASSUMPTIONS

Why are we so easily drawn into assuming a whole array of other things about people based merely on the way they look? Remember when some of us were attending high school and the thing about our long hair? Or the attitudes and belief systems we ascribe to people based on their style of dress? How about today's black clothes, steel chains, pierced body parts, creative tattoos, and purple hair?

We do it to ourselves. I was doing it to myself the other day, looking at Mr. and Mrs. Thirty-Something. I was doing it to them too. But it didn't last long.

MY BASIS FOR JOY

My assumptions didn't last long because I have another much more useful standard of self-worth and self-actualization, a better gauge for understanding who I really am. My joy meter relies on my certain knowledge that God loves me unconditionally, my awareness of the Creator's acceptance—unqualified and complete. I know I'd feel that way driving a Rolls-Royce or riding in a city bus; wearing my favorite boat shoes or that six-hundred-dollar silk jacket I tried on the other day; eating dinner at the Cheesecake Factory on our anniversary, down at the soup kitchen, or on the sidewalk outside the Salvation Army.

I really don't know anything about that good-looking couple in the sparkling new sports car. They may well be happy, genuine, and balanced people. I hope so. But what I do know is clear. I know that Christmas Day will eventually get here. I know that I will stumble and God will pick me up yet again. I know that Christ is born. I know that God loves me. And I know Jesus. I know that my life has such meaning and purpose that it overwhelms me sometimes. I know that because Christ died, I can be whole, and I can feel that wholeness nourishing my life in so many ways.

I also know, to paraphrase the verse in 2 Timothy, who it is that I have been depending on, and I am absolutely convinced beyond a shadow of a doubt that he has both the power and the purpose to follow through on all the promises he has made on my behalf. Because I know all of these things, I am richly blessed.

CERTAINTY, JOY, AND STRENGTH

Certainty like that always brings genuine peace and unqualified joy in the following forms:

- the assurance of God's personal love;
- the strength of God's unfailing Christmas promise;
- the sureness of faithfulness;
- the love of my family;
- my personal understanding that I am heir to the promises of God's kingdom.

There is great joy in contemplating the solid truths that God's Christmas intervention makes possible, the stuff we know we can always count on, the wholeness and the peace that can be a part of our lives, the rich blessings of God's covenant commitment to us.

REALITY

But knowing all that does little, if anything, to change the difficult circumstances that characterize the real lives of real people, lives often defined by distress and pain. Such understanding will not make our children like one another, and it will not make unhappy relationships tranquil again. Christmas will not pay the bills, slow down busy schedules, or remove fear regarding security or peace. Our certainty will not stop terrorists from targeting innocent people, and it will not bring people like Osama bin Laden to justice any sooner.

However—and this is critical—a deeply held certainty regarding the fundamental relationship of God's love to the small details of our lives—as real people who experience real problems—will give us a measure of strength and peace that is crucial. Such certainty empowers us, standing firmly between us and the specter of defeat; and certainty brings joy. The joy of the Lord is my strength.

- "Do not be grieved, for the joy of the LORD is your strength" (Neh. 8:10).
- "The LORD is my strength and my shield; in him my heart trusts; so I am helped, and my heart exults, and with my song I give thanks to him" (Ps. 28:7).
- "Rejoice in the Lord always; again I will say, Rejoice" (Phil. 4:4).

I AM PERSUADED

I am certain; I am confident; I am convinced; I am assured; I am positive. I am so many things that give me power and deep joy. I am persuaded.

Back in the 1930s, my late grandfather Fred Maul often traveled on business by rail. English trains in that day were sectioned into compartments with six or eight facing seats. During one such journey, conversation in my grandfather's compartment turned to religion.

"Of what persuasion are you?" one man asked, in the early twentieth-century vernacular for church or denomination.

"I'm Catholic," the first gentleman replied.

"Baptist," said another.

"Pentecostal," stated a third.

"Methodist" and "Church of England" rounded out the circle.

Eventually everyone looked at my grandfather, who was the last to show his denominational hand. Fred Maul smiled gently, the story goes, turned to the Bible he had removed from his coat pocket, and carefully read the following words: "I am persuaded, that neither death, nor life, nor angels, nor principalities, nor powers, nor things present, nor things to come, nor height, nor depth, nor any other creature, shall be able to separate us from the love of God, which is in Christ Jesus our Lord" (Rom. 8:38-39, KJV).

That is Christmas joy. That is "the good treasure" the Timothy passage tells us we are entrusted to guard. The assurance of Romans 8 is much more compelling than any apple-red BMW convertible, even on a balmy Florida evening.

Prayer: Thank you, God, for Christmas joy. Thank you for loving me with the amazing heart-knowledge of your certainty in my often uncertain life. Victory is always there when we acknowledge how much you love us and how generously you validate every detail of our lives. Amen.

MONDAY

TURTLES AND OTHER MOMENTS OF SWEET MAGIC

All things came into being through him, and without him not one thing came into being. What has come into being in him was life, and the life was the light of all people.

—John 1:3-4

Christmas is a lot like a great family vacation. The festive atmosphere, the unbounded optimism, the simple joy of being together—it all works to produce a magical tingling in the air I can only describe in terms of joy. It's the sense of joy wrapped in discovery: new meaning, giving, generosity, or gratitude; uncovering another nugget of God's love; breaking through to uncharted levels in the realm of faith; or the unearthing of newfound pleasure.

On the other hand, a family vacation sometimes makes me think about Christmas: the peace that comes when we remove ourselves from day-to-day routine; the hope for family relationships; the love that always comes through when we have time to be relaxed together; and then—most especially—the experience of joy.

Somewhere, somehow, on vacation, one particular day or hour moves our family beyond the realm of the mundane and into the province of enchantment. It may be a serendipitous night in a starlit canyon; our early morning balloon ride in Sedona; a deep father-son moment on the craggy coast of Scotland; or that unforgettable day we stood on the deck of the Johnston Ridge Observatory and watched

Mount St. Helens belch an impressive cloud of ash into the blue Washington sky.

One summer we simply went to the beach. We had a great time, and the experience was relaxing, invigorating, fun. But one day had been fraught with the kind of family tensions we had intended to leave behind. We approached the end of the evening disappointed and cranky. Around midnight Rebekah and I climbed to the boardwalk for a redemptive look at the ocean. Suddenly, through an unexpected break in the clouds, a full moon bathed the breaking waves in a silvery light. There, in the broken surf, we saw an enormous black shape begin to haul itself laboriously onto the sand.

"It's a turtle!" Rebekah yelled. "Let's get the children."

Who cared if they were in bed? This was important stuff.

Andrew had his *Florida Reptiles and Amphibians* book and a small flashlight at hand, ready for just such an occurrence. Naomi emerged sleepy, reluctant, and wrapped in a blanket.

There we stood, our small family huddled together in the full moon and the cool breeze to witness a miracle. Slowly and deliberately, the gargantuan turtle (four feet across and six hundred pounds) pulled herself across a full fifty feet of sand and up to the dunes where she paused to gather strength before digging a two-foot-deep hole with her back flippers.

Alternately breathing and digging (loggerheads use the same muscle group for both activities), the great sea creature carefully arranged her space before laying the precious eggs and painstakingly covering her nest. We watched her lumber back to the sea, transforming miraculously into a graceful, fluid swimmer once she left the beach behind.

What a miracle! What a moment of sweet magic! What an experience of intimacy with the wonders of our generous and magnificent world!

The next day we saw dolphins playing off the dock, and I made a lot of noise clearing the water when I thought an approaching manatee was a dangerous shark! There were cookouts, day trips, and epic games of Scrabble. But this vacation was the vacation of the turtle; it always will be, and I'm captured as always with a sense of amazement and gratitude for the beauty and the depth of the marvels of creation.

"God saw everything that he had made, and indeed, it was very good. And there was evening and there was morning, the sixth day" (Gen. 1:31).

THIS GOOD EARTH

Quite often we allow ourselves to focus on the negative. We easily talk about how rotten and sinful and decayed this world is. We like to point out depravity, and some of us even rub our hands together as if Christians should relish the prospect of this world "going to hell in a handbasket," an event that might hasten the ultimate culmination of the story of history.

Paul talks about the entire creation groaning in confusion and looking with anticipation for the Children of Light—that's us—to begin doing something positive about the situation: "For the creation waits with eager longing for the revealing of the children of God; for the creation was subjected to futility, not of its own will but by the will of the one who subjected it, in hope that the creation itself will be set free from its bondage to decay and will obtain the freedom of the glory of the children of God" (Rom. 8:19-21).

Something fundamentally joy-filled about Christmas reminds me of how God created a good earth.

But something fundamentally joy-filled about Christmas reminds me of how God created a good earth. This world is not so much a dark and evil realm as it is a confused and misguided place. That thought—and it's a thought that gains a lot of credibility at Christmas—gives me more than a little joy. In the first chapter of Genesis God repeats a refrain of affirmation: "It is good," "Nice work," "I really think I like that," "Great day's work," "Gotta give myself props!" "God saw everything that he had made, and indeed, it was very good" (Gen. 1:31).

People are inherently and fundamentally good, even accounting for original sin. God created people; God doesn't do bad work. We all have the raw ingredients to shine, and Christmas proves that reality in so many ways: ordinary people empowered to do extraordinary deeds; generosity and selflessness and love. Literally billions of dollars and incalculable hours donated to more charitable causes than most of us could imagine.

The famous Dickens character Ebenezer Scrooge is a good case in point. The author devised a masterful plot using "ghosts" of Christmas Past, Christmas Present, and Christmas Future to illustrate the progress of one egocentric, corrupt man from self-absorption and spite into the glorious light of Christmas joy.

This "Spirit" of Christmas that so many people—even nonbelievers—like to talk about (especially in the shopping malls) has the authority to resurrect the deep truth that God already created. Such re-creation is the purview of none other than the Holy Spirit. The fact that this "Christmas Spirit" works so effectively testifies to the truth that God implanted the raw substance of pure joy in each one of us. It's the potentiality to experience and to revel in God's great gladness, a delight that is creation itself.

Prayer: Thank you, God, for the opportunity to share in the great gladness of your joy. We pray that our Advent journey will be filled with moments of affirmation and of love. Your great gift of Jesus, Immanuel overwhelms us sometimes, and we are glad. Amen.

TUESDAY

JOY IN BELIEVING—ROCK THE WORLD!

May the God of hope fill you with all joy and peace in believing, so that you may abound in hope by the power of the Holy Spirit.
—Romans 15:13

One of the best things about family road trips with small children was the great storytelling. Rebekah is a master storyteller, and she has a barrel-load to pull from. The best tales were family legends, and between the Alexanders on her dad's side and her mother's Perkins clan, let me tell you there were characters to spare.

My favorite rogue relative has to be Rebekah's nineteenth-century great-great-great aunt, or thereabouts. We believe she was the only woman (or the last woman . . . or the best-looking woman) to be hanged as a horse thief in the state of Tennessee. Then there's the courageous Hezekiah Alexander, who signed the Mecklenburg Declaration of 1775; the orange farmer who lost a fortune in Florida to a late frost in 1892 (and another fortune to gambling a decade later), and the Duncan who walked back to Georgia after the Battle of Gettysburg because—contrary to that other relative—he refused to take a farmer's only horse.

Then there are the stories my wife made up. I especially enjoy the tall tale that got her in trouble in elementary school. She told her classmates that her dad—a Presbyterian minister—and his two brothers went out and robbed a bank when they were young. One uncle, she said, took the money and ran to Brazil; her father (who drove the getaway car in most versions) found the Lord and entered the ministry. Her other uncle—she told her wide-eyed classmates, who of course swallowed every word—is rotting in jail to this day.

She explains that she had grown weary of retelling the more-mundane truth of the three brothers who all attended seminary before entering the ministry; she had merely tweaked the essential facts. Charles served as a missionary in Brazil for more than twenty years; her dad pastored churches in Georgia and then Florida; and George—the youngest—worked in prison chaplaincy until he was appointed superintendent of a federal penitentiary in Ohio.

But best of all were the stories we told on ourselves. "Tell us about when you were a little girl, Mama." And, "Make Daddy tell one about when he was a little boy."

We always took a book or two or three for the road. We started the Children's Classics series when Andrew and Naomi were young, and we went through scores of volumes, such as *Kidnapped, Heidi, Robin Hood, King Arthur,* and *Treasure Island.* One of my favorite road trips took in Washington, DC. Driving was adventurous fun, especially pre–satellite-navigation in a busy city well known for not allowing anyone to turn left—ever! Right turns were more acceptable, and I vividly remember getting tantalizingly close to destinations, then carefully spiraling my way clockwise in a series of ever-tightening circles until I hit my target.

The National Cathedral was one landmark well worth the effort. Since I was raised in Europe, I found the spectacle of a shiny new (relatively speaking) Gothic-styled edifice intriguing on many levels. One exhibit in particular caught my imagination. Hanging on an obscure wall in a room off the beaten path I found a photograph of the cathedral site taken not many years after the cornerstone was laid in 1907. Architect Henry Vaughan knew he would not live to see the completion of the project, yet he had fleshed out the photograph by etching clear lines to represent the appearance of a magnificent church. The skeletal structure rose above and around the foundations on the sepia-toned plate as a testimony to a faith and belief that saw clearly.

Vaughan's death in 1917 marked the end of his role. The National Cathedral was not officially finished until September 29, 1990. Standing in the annex that day, I peered into the glass-covered photograph and could almost see Vaughan's reflection, a twinkle in his eye revealing the relationship between honest belief and genuine joy.

CANTERBURY TALES

The National Cathedral reminds me of the more ancient edifice at Canterbury, in the south of England. Most of that building was constructed between the years 1070 and 1498. I grew up just a few miles down the road. The famous church seemed to reach back into history, towering over the crowded narrow streets with a medieval presence. In many respects the great sanctuary had become more museum than house of worship. The massive nave seemed to me at times like a huge tombstone erected in memory to a Christian witness long since sputtered out. Until one evening in the early 1970s. On that occasion several thousand of my friends rocked the place with the sacred contemporary musical *Come Together*, written by Jimmy and Carol Owens. The band took residence on the stone steps leading up to the choir, and the worship space was jammed with young people.

I'm talking guitar, bass, brass, piano, Hammond organ, and a nice, crisp drum set; microphones, jeans, T-shirts, "Jesus-freak" paraphernalia, flowers in hair, and sandals. Canterbury Cathedral was bursting to overflowing with people; God's praise literally rang from the pre-Reformation rafters; and my spirit burst wide open with joy.

Many years later I traveled back to Canterbury with Rebekah. After walking the narrow streets and enjoying lunch in a cozy restaurant built into the cathedral wall, we made our way to the great church. As we walked slowly down one of the transepts, I fell into conversation with an elderly priest. I shared my experience as a teen and asked him if he had heard of the event.

The elderly cleric's eyes lit up and he smiled. "I was there," he said. "It was as if this wonderful building was being filled to the brim with exactly the kind of praise it was designed to witness." He took my hand, and a peaceful expression passed over his face. "I have never known such joy," he said.

At that moment a young man made his way to one of the lecterns, opened a book, and began to pray in a quiet voice. As he finished, he extended his hands by way of invitation and—slowly—began to recite the Lord's Prayer. It was a summer Saturday, and Canterbury was crowded with tourists from all around the world. Still, in a miracle of devotion and unity, all conversation ceased by the end of the first phrase. By the time the words "hallowed be thy name" were half-uttered, the majority of visitors fell into cadence, each praying in their own tongue, each with a unique intonation that blended in symphonic harmony and absolute clarity.

I believe we rocked the place again that day.

Joy is the heartbeat of a world united, joined in heartfelt worship and self-giving service. Joy is believing. Joy is seeing God's hand at work with simplicity and purpose. "May the God of hope fill you with all joy and peace in believing" (Rom. 15:13).

Prayer: Our Father in heaven, hallowed be your name; your kingdom come, your will be done, on earth as it is in heaven. Give us today our daily bread. Forgive us our sins as we forgive those who sin against us. Save us from the time of trial and deliver us from evil. For the kingdom, the power, and the glory are yours, now and forever. Amen.

WEDNESDAY

THE GIFT YOU'VE ALWAYS WANTED

When they saw that the star had stopped, they were overwhelmed with joy. On entering the house, they saw the child with Mary his mother; and they knelt down and paid him homage. Then, opening their treasure chests, they offered him gifts of gold, frankincense, and myrrh.

—Matthew 2:10-11

Just a few days and counting till the day before the night before Christmas. This is when seasonal excitement begins to settle in on me for keeps. It's butterflies-in-the-stomach-catch-my-breath level anticipation, and it isn't likely to let up much, if at all, between now and "O Holy Night."

Such a gut-level response is part of the package I wouldn't miss, but I have to avoid one mistake I make all too easily. If I don't watch myself closely, I tend to romanticize Christmas to the extent of imagining something synthetic. Then, before I know it, I've turned December 25 into a holiday without substance, one that accomplishes nothing more than stoking nostalgia, distracting from reality, and moving the economy forward.

Mea culpa. I am as guilty as anyone in this regard. Sometimes I wonder if I'm maybe more receptive to the smell of spice tea than the bitter bouquet of frankincense or myrrh; more attached to the aroma of fresh baking bread than the baser fumes of the stable; more prepared to celebrate stockings in front of a warm fire than a cold night behind a crowded inn.

Is this the Advent of Christ? Or a Hollywood set I have constructed to entertain myself? Do I avoid disquieting truth and assign bit parts to

Jesus and the other characters? Or am I preparing to celebrate the coming of my King?

So this week I will be asking myself a few challenging questions. What role should I assign God this year? What happens when I draw the curtain on the tableau? Am I a spectator or a participant?

What would I have left if:

- Someone took away my tree?
- All the brightly wrapped presents disappeared?
- Police removed the lights from the front of my house?
- The singing of seasonal songs was banned?
- Any reference to Christmas was purged from the public record?
- The FDA decreed a moratorium on any food item destined to tip my calorie total north of the recommended daily allowance?

Well, apart from getting appallingly close to what some people would have us believe America should look like once they erase religion from public life, we would still have pretty much everything that matters. This is the celebration our culture dances around but seldom gets too close to each December. And if the lords of this world took away the elements they believe represent Christmas, then—truth is—they wouldn't really do much damage at all.

When God took the unprecedented and outrageous step of entering this finite world as a helpless child, God addressed exactly what humankind was missing. Inasmuch as we believe we can take care of what we lack via lights, trees, jolly elves, and expensive presents, we risk insulating ourselves from Jesus, the only focus of authentic substance present in the entire festive season.

I'm going to *cut to the chase*:

- All Christmas trees are artificial without nails and a crown of thorns.
- Even the most expensive present fails to cover the cost of missing the Gift.
- Fancy icicle lights don't hold a candle to the Light of the world.
- Forget "Jingle Bell Rock" or "chestnuts roasting on an open fire,"

the only way "I'll Be Home for Christmas" is through "Silent night, holy night, Son of God, love's pure light."

- I may well go beyond the FDA's recommended calorie intake this weekend, but I guarantee there is only one way I'll be truly satisfied.

Something remarkable happened that night in Bethlehem. Something remarkable can happen this year too. It's "the dawn of redeeming grace" ("Silent Night"). I call it our opportunity to finally end the drought and get "the gift we've always wanted."

Merry Christmas.

Prayer: Help me to understand the essential truth of your coming, Lord. Give me clarity, and grant us all authentic joy. Amen.

THURSDAY

FULL TO THE VERY BRIM! HEALING JOY

Jesus said to them, "Fill the jars with water." And they filled them up to the brim. . . . "Everyone serves the good wine first, and then the inferior wine after the guests have become drunk. But you have kept the good wine until now."

—John 2:7, 10

My daughter Naomi's wedding—just a few days ago as I write—easily ranks as one of the most genuinely joy-filled occasions of my life. Wanting to see our children happy may be a cliché, but, truism or not, when our offspring are happy, there's simply nothing like it. And when they're blissfully, radiantly happy—then pretty much all we can do is to settle back and cry.

I have always wondered what my primary emotion would be when I walked my daughter down the aisle. I'd been told to expect "bitter-sweet," "poignant," "tender," or maybe "a little sad." But instead, I was bursting, out-and-out joyful, filled to the brim.

As my wife and I watch the happy couple grow together and observe the kind of authentic gladness they share, it's impossible to miss the relationship between pure love and genuine healing. Healing not just for them but for the entire family.

It's all very complex, this "raising a family" adventure, but it's precisely the contrast between the hurting of brokenness and the healing of restoration that adds up to the unspeakable joy our family experiences today. The anatomy of the process is a lot like the quality of joy God made possible through Christmas. Jesus was born into a world defined by the pain of separation, and reconciliation becomes possible through the healing gift of Jesus—the Savior who is Christ the Lord.

Prayer Leads to Healing

The guest list for Naomi and Craig's Friday-night rehearsal dinner was telling: Craig's family—not a huge crowd; then my small family; plus Rebekah's plentiful assortment of siblings; and filled out with various nieces and nephews. Next, our church staff were invited; some close friends; and Naomi's maid of honor, Lacey. Finally, we included a select representation from Rebekah's first pastorate in Pensacola, most notably the original "covenant group," the first small group Rebekah and I made a commitment with so many years ago.

Most of the folk who gathered for dinner that night had worn actual holes in the knees of their pants praying our small family through several years of darkness and doubt, times when we had been unable to see anything much more than hopelessness and pain. We'd gone through counseling, practiced "tough love," watched from the sidelines as poor decisions led to worse outcomes, and prayed relentlessly for glimpses of hope. Yet,

Sometimes raising our children is straightforward; other times it's the most difficult task in the world.

like the children of Israel drifting ever farther from the reach of the Creator who loved them so much, the summary of it all was too often impasse, disappointment, confusion, and pain.

Sometimes raising our children is straightforward; other times it's the most difficult task in the world. Always, parenting is a privilege, a constant opportunity to rely completely on God. These folks at the rehearsal dinner had all played the part of God-with-us in countless different ways over several pivotal years.

Alaska on Ice

The year 2006 started out well, with lots of encouragement and several steps forward. Not only had our prodigal daughter made some constructive choices, but we had experienced some family reconciliation too. Then, real joy in the midst of challenge, my family lined up an epic vacation for the early summer. "The Alaska Cruise" was all set to go, but Naomi had an important new job and almost couldn't make the giant floating hotel that steamed out from Seattle on a remarkably sunny May 4.

Meanwhile, Craig—who had almost ended up on another ship at another time before the greater designs of providence steered him to Seattle—was already on board as assistant cruise director. He was looking for change and ready for adventure after working his way through college in New England.

I have this great photograph: eleven immediate family members gathered on the Seattle dockside, May 2006, with a huge Holland America vessel in the background. "Look carefully: Craig's in the picture somewhere," we love to say. And he was; unbeknownst to any of us, unimagined as a player in our lives, and working somewhere between decks. But he was on God's mind, and so was God's beloved child Naomi.

THE TOAST

A reception room full of joy. Reunions, catching up, laughter, prayer, and tears. Dinner, dessert, coffee—and then silence as Craig's dad "dinged" his glass to quiet the buzz. He shared a few words of greeting, offered a brief toast, then signaled to me. It was my turn.

"Naomi and Craig," I began. "That certainly has a nice ring to it. Craig and Naomi Campbell? Nice. You know, I think I'm going to like the sound of that too.

"This is a great moment," I said, "this merging together of individuals . . . of families . . . of history . . . of traditions . . . of lives . . . of futures . . . of love . . . of hopes, of possibilities, and of dreams. It's the kind of event that every parent eventually expects, sort of prays for, maybe even dreads a little, and certainly always wonders about in the back of their mind."

I paused, took a long and deliberate swig from my coffee cup, and glanced around the room at so many friends, so many people who loved us from the bottom of their generous hearts. I continued:

"Naomi, we had some guys picked out for you when you were three years old! Then you had a bunch of different guys picked out for you— off and on for a number of years. But God, I believe, had one particular man in mind since before the foundation of time.

"I've shared this thought before, but I think it bears repeating, because a lot of people get the beautiful design of God's providence confused with the dark inevitability of fatalism—and they're way off the mark.

"Here's the way I see *providence*: When God's perfect will—the loving intention and the purpose of the Creator—intersects with our conscious choice to respond in faith . . . then that point of intersection is providence. And believe me when I tell you that is a powerful moment.

"Craig and Naomi meeting on the big floating smorgasbord off the coast of Alaska? Now that's providence. The confluence of these two families—the Maul/Alexander bunch and the Campbell/Zuccato clan— this too is a special moment."

I glanced over at Craig's parents. I knew they were wondering what on earth I was going to say next!

"My neighbor summed things up pretty well recently when he said this: 'Hey, Derek, our daughter is going to turn twenty in just a few more years. When she does, I need to borrow that catalog you found Craig in; because Debbie and I are going to want one just like him!'"

Everybody chuckled. And everyone smiled too. It was the kind of laughing that emerges not from some corny joke but from the welling up of joy. There was joy loose in the room, and it was getting all over everything. I looked at my daughter, and I addressed her alone:

"Back in 2003, Naomi, when you graduated from high school, I published an 'Open Letter to My Daughter' in the *Tampa Tribune*. The column finished like this: 'And we love you. We love you in the knowledge that though our love is imperfect, flawed by our own weakness and fear, God's love is pure, welcoming, and relentless. Where our love may not see clearly, God's love cuts through the fog with clarity and with truth. Where our love is strong, God's love is stronger. And where our love in its imperfection may seem sometimes to hurt, God's love—which is perfect—will always heal.'"

I almost cried. Sometimes I can't read my own writing.

"This, Naomi, is one more great moment of healing." And then I did cry.

I turned to her almost husband. "Craig," I said, "welcome to the family. 'God,' as Jesse Alexander (Rebekah's youngest brother) is wont to say, 'is good.'

"I'll add the following: God is certainly extraordinarily gracious too."

I lifted my glass: "Joy, then, to Naomi and to Craig. Joy everlasting to one and to all."

Prayer: "If then there is any encouragement in Christ, any consolation from love, any sharing in the Spirit, any compassion and sympathy, make my joy complete: be of the same mind, having the same love, being in full accord and of one mind. Do nothing from selfish ambition or conceit, but in humility regard others as better than yourselves. Let each of you look not to your own interests, but to the interests of others. Let the same mind be in you that was in Christ Jesus."* Amen.

* Philippians 2:1-5

CHRISTMAS EVE
A LITTLE LIGHT FOR THE NEW YEAR

But the angel said to them, "Do not be afraid; for see—I am bringing you good news of great joy for all the people: to you is born this day in the city of David a Savior, who is the Messiah, the Lord. This will be a sign for you: you will find a child wrapped in bands of cloth and lying in a manger."

—Luke 2:10-12

Today has to be my absolute favorite of all the special days. Christmas Eve is joy multiplied. It's a day loaded with the stardust, dreams, and the deep magic of all our accumulated wonder.

It seems sometimes that the echo of all our childhood joys covers December 24. The goodwill possible in all people colors even the mundane gestures of common life. Don't you feel the tingling in the air? Isn't it true that even the honks of cars, the bark of neighborhood dogs, and the noises of business sound friendlier today?

I even enjoy Christmas Eve shopping, so I typically pick up a few small stocking-stuffer gifts at the last minute simply because I can't get enough of the festive atmosphere. I like the sense of immediacy, the urgency, the unapologetic Christmas high.

Every example of goodwill proclaims Christ's coming. Every genuine outbreak of "Christmas Spirit" speaks God's blessing. Every gracious act of love, gesture of peace, and inkling of hope proclaims the witness of the shepherds. Each resounding experience of joy cries out with passion the reality of God's creative and redeeming love. What a dark world this would be without Christ! What an empty festival of winter would remain if God had not so loved this world.

LIGHTS, CAMERA, ACTION!

One of my friends told me recently that "it just wouldn't be Christmas" if he didn't sit down at some point to watch the Burl Ives animated classic *Rudolph the Red-Nosed Reindeer* (1964).

Well, to each his own. My must-see seasonal videos run more along the lines of *A Christmas Story, It's a Wonderful Life, Miracle on 34th Street*, and almost any rendition of the Dickens classic *A Christmas Carol*.

But there's really not a deal-breaker on the list. Over the years I've missed out on many elements I once considered critical, but of course they're not. Sometimes we get "what I'm used to" confused with "what really counts," and we all turn out to be die-hard conservatives when it comes to nostalgia. What matters is Jesus, bottom line; anything else is dressing. It's critical we keep things in perspective.

Regardless, most of us do have something special we look forward to, some aspect of celebration that best sums up the whole ball of wax when it comes to Christmas joy. These are the moments of pure epiphany where all the celebration, all the hope, all the meaning, and all the excitement seem to be wrapped up in a single instant.

IT HAS TO BE WORSHIP

My moment often happens in church, usually about halfway through the candlelighting on Christmas Eve. The sanctuary is completely dark, with the exception of the Christ Candle, and I enjoy the privilege of standing with the choir, slightly elevated, playing "Silent Night" on my acoustic guitar. It's a moment I anticipate every year.

The minister takes the flame and lights several candles, each one held by a leader in the church. Then, spreading out through the congregation, the elders carry their lights to the end of each row. Hundreds of people, young and old, touch wick to wick with naked flame.

It is then, with the light still reproducing but not yet complete, that it comes to me afresh why I love Christmas so much. In a world under siege by those who would seek to condemn; on a planet where it is so much easier to say what we are against than what we are for; in a society where the loudest sound we hear is often cynicism, argument, and complaint; where the clamor of war at times can be overwhelming—there is a more excellent way; there is a path that strives to illuminate rather than to destroy. There is a light we can pass, a light by which we can brighten every human heart we choose to touch, and bring healing to every place where God's grace directs us to serve.

There is a more excellent way; there is a path that strives to illuminate rather than to destroy.

The Light of Christmas Joy

Because of Christmas, we have received the gift of recognizing what happens when darkness is confronted by light. This particular evening, looking out over a multitude of people drawn from the shadows by the compelling light of the gospel, I find myself thinking about the coming new year.

The faces of a family I know to be struggling are captured in the glow, and I pray God's peace. A lost teenager smiles into her candle, so I ask God to show her the way home. My mind wanders to the Middle East, and I notice four children moving their lips in prayer—their father is serving in Iraq. I realize how much stronger love is than fear and how powerful are its messengers once released—equipped—into the world.

For me such moments of insight also serve to set the stage perfectly for the coming new year, a time often associated with a kind of post-holiday letdown, defeat, and unreasonable sadness as people contemplate the difficulties they had happily pushed aside. Decorations come down; lights hang, unlit, well into the January grayness; hope is stuffed into cardboard boxes; and the joy that held Advent truth so eloquently too readily dissolves into pain.

That is why I am so grateful that—once the candles are lit—my guitar playing is joined by hundreds of voices singing, ever so tenderly, "Son of God, love's pure light; radiant beams from thy holy face, with the dawn of redeeming grace. . . ."*

And the grace-filled congregation leaves the sanctuary, carrying a light that will never fade in the dreary January days that can so easily disappoint.

Prayer: Please help us, loving and generous God, to remember the genuine joy we feel on Christmas Eve. We believe, with confidence, that the spiritual connectedness we experience at the height of celebration can be ours always, in the sure knowledge of your patient love. Your great gift humbles us, gracious God, and we are filled with joy. Amen.

* Joseph Mohr (1792–1848), trans. John F. Young

CHRISTMAS DAY!
JOY: UNPACKING GOD'S LOVE

> The people who walked in darkness
> > have seen a great light;
> those who lived in a land of deep darkness—
> > on them light has shined.
> You have multiplied the nation,
> > you have increased its joy.
>
> > —Isaiah 9:2-3

Here's a great question: What exactly are we unwrapping this fine Christmas morning?

I like the way pastor Bob Gibbs (St. Andrew's United Methodist Church, Brandon, Florida) talks about God's love. "It's foundational to everything," he said. "God accepts all of us; that's an incredible assurance and peace but also a responsibility. It's basic, but we're still unpacking that. I believe we are thoroughly loved and accepted by God. The grace of God, that's where it starts."

Regardless, there's probably a colossal bunch of loot stuffed under our trees and waiting to be unwrapped. But if we're not excited about "unpacking" God's remarkable gift, if we're not reengaging grace, if we're not taking this opportunity to simply breathe in the generous love of the Lord of Creation . . . then we're missing the very best part. This Christmas, having already unpacked Advent along the way, let's not miss the most complete gift of all.

The Journey There Is More Than Half the Fun

Late Christmas Eve, after my family returns home from church, Rebekah and I quietly walk our neighborhood; we do it every year. The streets, lined with paper-bag luminaries, still glow subtly. Inside our house, the kettle is boiling for hot tea, and our young-adult children are waiting for me to read "The Night Before Christmas." "Next year," they always tell me, "we'll be too old."

But we take our time. We have, after all, been preparing reflectively through four weeks of deliberate Advent. We plan to be truly ready for the coming of the King.

Twelve Days

When we wake up, it's Christmas morning; "Advent" is officially over. But far from winding up the celebrations, the Twelve Days of Christmas officially begin on December 25. Living the truth about Christmas is another opportunity to affirm the countercultural thrust of the gospel; as Christ-followers we can continue to take our lead from Jesus instead of the world.

But we live in a civilization driven to honor commerce, the most demanding of our gods. The instant the last gift is unwrapped, the entire machine runs out of steam and pretty much deflates, right there on the living room floor. And that, my Advent traveling companions, is a sad, sad reality that we simply cannot accommodate or continue to support.

People all over the world experience postholiday depression, sometimes as early as first-light Christmas morning. However, when a socially leveraged gift binge becomes the defining moment, when weeks of buildup lead inescapably to one anticlimactic half hour, then what else could possibly remain but disillusionment and bitter disappointment?

Rituals of Grace

For the past twenty years we've eschewed the holiday dinner convention and instead prepared a light Christmas brunch. I always create something extraordinary, but I do the work ahead of time. Christmas morning, the casserole—or sometimes a variety of quiches—goes in the oven around nine o'clock. That's when we pour the coffee, pass out a few cinnamon rolls, read the Christmas story, and share family devotions.

Yes, we begin the day in simple worship. Devotion creates the best context for owning Christmas joy. Then, one at a time and without a rush, we open our gifts.

Later, Rebekah bakes fresh bread. I add a bowl of fruit, throw in some special touches like real cream for the coffee, and we all settle down to a joy-filled brunch before enjoying family for the balance of the day.

Christmas, stress-free: loads of opportunity to play as a family, kitchen cleanup at a minimum, relaxed conversation. All this couched in the context of spiritual blessing. It's been twenty-some years now, and we haven't looked back. Today the kids are grown, but they still bring all kinds of friends into the house Christmas Day; in fact, we all do.

The focus is Jesus. God's great gift unwrapped for Christmas. "The people who walked in darkness have seen a great light" (Isa. 9:2).

Prayer: Thank you so very much, God, for the amazing generosity you have extended in Christmas; thank you for your light. You are our God of hope, the only way to peace, the Lord of love, and the bringer of joy. How can we possibly communicate the depth of our gratitude unless we accept the gift of Jesus, humbly and without reservation? We do accept your gift, God. Please guide us on the way. Amen.

Epilogue

V ery often, starting around the last few days and counting before Christmas, otherwise downcast people begin to light up from the inside. Something changes—something fundamental—and even confirmed Scrooges are seen to smile, wave, and hold the door for strangers.

"He's caught the Christmas Spirit," people will say. Or, "Too bad she's not really this nice." And, "Enjoy it while it lasts; in a couple of days he'll be back to normal."

But here's what I think: the goodwill, the pleasantry, and the gentle light shining from deep inside these folk is nothing short of 100 percent natural. What's abnormal is the dysfunction; what's wide of God's mark are the other 360-plus days; what's uncalled for is this broken world's unrelenting pain.

As Christ-followers we have this power to turn things around; we have this extraordinary opportunity to plug people back into normal. We can be the people who have the courage to *truly* unpack Christmas.